Mostly Untrue Stories

by

Rick Seidenwurm

Mostly Untrue Stories

Author: Rick Seidenwurm

For permission, please contact:
    Rick Seidenwurm
    rickseidenwurm@gmail.com

Cover design by Kari Cureton

Book layout/design by David Larson

Table of Contents

Thanks

To Carol Seidenwurm, who encouraged me to write every step of the way and appears prominently in some of these stories.

To Susan Horowitz, my partner and emergency contact, who helped edit these stories and felt free to tell me when she thought I crossed the line.

To Amy Seidenwurm and Rob Seidenwurm, two of the very best readers I know.

To my writing guru, Judy Reeves, who invited me to join an advanced writing group when I thought I was a pretty raw rookie.

To the members of that original group, Jenn, Judy G, Nancy, Rich, and Scott. I still have and treasure your edits.

To my second writing group, John, Kim, and Victoria. We shared lots of insights, pizza, and wine.

To my layout team Dave Larson and Kari Cureton. You made the process much easier than I feared.

Dedication

I'm thrilled to dedicate *Mostly Untrue Stories* to my mother Lil Seidenwurm, who encouraged me to read and to love the printed and spoken word. During toilet training, she had me memorize and recite the Gettysburg Address. She always had a book by her side and transcribed classic novels into Braille in her spare time. Thanks Mom!

Where I'm From

I'm from LongIsland and I useta tawk like dis.

I'm from parents much shorter than me who said B+ was
not good enough.

I'm from the odor of bacon grease in the morning and lox
on Sundays.

I'm from the very sour cherry tree which took up half our
backyard and wasn't safe to climb.

I'm from shooting hoops two hours every day so I wouldn't
get picked last in the chooseup.

I'm from wearing short pants years after the cool guys had
graduated to chinos.

I'm one of the only people I know who will admit to a
happy childhood.

I've been called The Wurm, Rico, The Rickster, The Little
Shit, and Pop-Pop.

I'm from New York when it was a tough place and eye
contact was to be avoided.

I'm from pushy in-laws who knew what was best for their
daughter and me.

I'm from a great job that I loved but kept me away too
much.

I'm from watching my son being born, shriveled gray body
emerging from a proud sweaty Carol.

I'm from San Diego, where my daughter Amy got amnesia
the day we arrived.

Where eye contact is OK and even encouraged.

Where I knew someone who was murdered, pistol
whipped to death.

Where I hit a perfect golf shot and watched it go in the
hole.

Where I finally witnessed a green flash.

I'm from horrible back pain, the taste of bile and the
stench of puke.

Mostly Untrue Stories

I'm from incredible elation, the taste of lobster and the
spicy scent of Calla lilies.
I'm from seeing my kids achieve and grow and make
mistakes,
And from finally learning to let them find their own ways.

I'm from watching Carol wither away from cancer,
While somehow believing she would get better.
I'm from singing to her as she gasped that last breath
Knowing she couldn't hear a word.

I'm from meeting Susan and falling in love again, so much
less complicated this time.
I'm from a condo on the beach where the waves roar 24/7.
I'm from a thousand friends or so and the chance to make
more every day.
I'm from the joy I get from giving back to the amazing
world I'm from.

Awakening

Danny awoke at 6:40 as he did every morning, no alarm required. He rolled out of bed, naked as a jaybird as his Dad would have said, and realized he was not alone. He was pretty sure that the large lump submerged under his royal blue comforter was named Debbie. He'd met her at the Speakeasy Pub in downtown Boulder last night and they'd connected, ending up with a pretty decent roll in the hay given the amount of alcohol each had thrown down.

But these mornings were always the awkward times, dealing with bathroom etiquette in his barely one-bedroom apartment, deciding whether to make a joke about her putting on yesterday's crumpled skirt and blouse and wearing them back to work, pondering whether to make toast and maybe even eggs or stick to coffee. A sound, halfway between a snore and a whimper, came from somewhere deep inside the still-very asleep Debbie. He plugged in the toaster.

He trotted into the bathroom, shut the door, peed, and brushed his teeth. *To flush or not to flush? Is it better to expose your urine to the gaze of the fair damsel or risk her premature awakening? What would Romeo have done?* He flushed and opened the door. Cool, she hadn't stirred. He slipped on his favorite jeans and guided a gray Polo over his head. His feet were bare. September in Boulder was wacky. It had been 82 degrees yesterday although the first snow could come anytime now.

The kitchen was spotless-- the maid had been there just yesterday. In his horny drunken stupor last night, Danny forgot to set the autobrew on his Cuisinart coffeemaker. Not a problem, it only took a minute or two. He carefully measured the water and the French Roast and switched the machine to on. The morning ritual continued as he flicked on the tiny 12-inch TV on the kitchen counter, his early morning companion since freshman year at Michigan State.

And there they were, the CNBC stock gurus, David the Brain Faber, wiseguy Joe Kernen, and Maria Bartiromo, the gorgeous Italian temptress with the turnoff Brooklyn accent. They looked worried, like maybe the market had taken a dive. But no, it was only about twenty minutes after the opening and the indexes were flat, according to the roll at the bottom of the screen. The Brain looked ten years older than yesterday as he repeated, as if for Danny's benefit, "We have received unconfirmed reports that an airplane, believed to be a small private plane, crashed a few minutes ago into the North Tower of the World Trade Center in New York. Please stay tuned to CNBC for further details as they become available."

Danny stared at the screen, waiting for someone to shout "April Fool" or "Gotcha". Nobody did. It was too bizarre to be real. How the fuck could a private plane get so off course and be so clueless as to crash into a skyscraper?

Danny dashed from kitchen to bedroom. "Wake up Debbie. You gotta see this. It's absolutely unbelievable."

A bleached blond head emerged from under the covers. Her dark blue eyelids opened a speck as she rolled from stomach to side, a pendulous breast leading the way, running interference for the rest of her body.

"Wha, wha, wha time is it? Whazammata?"

He switched on the bedroom TV and tuned to CNBC. The stock ticker was still running at the bottom, but the main screen showed fuzzy images of smoky downtown New York, morning commuters running this way and that, some toward the smoke and some away from it. Sirens screamed, an old woman with a cane mouthed a cry for help, and cops and firemen arrived at the scene, looking official but without a game plan.

Danny was sure the director or somebody had told the CNBC gang to appear calm, but they seemed terrified and couldn't hide it. Maria reported that the only damage was to the North Tower and tenants of the South Tower had been told by loudspeaker that the building was secure and there was no need to evacuate. Most of the tenants weren't obeying, judging from the swarms of people CNBC showed abandoning the South Tower and running like hell uptown or toward the Brooklyn Bridge. Danny thought he would have been halfway to Brooklyn by now if he worked there.

She was sitting up in bed now, but still looked half asleep. "Um, um, what the hell is going on? Uh, uh, Danny?"

"Some private plane just crashed into the World Trade Center. It's chaos, people running all over the place. This is fucking nuts."

And then the frantic cry of ' Omigod, another one', coming from somebody not an announcer, and there it was live and in color, a giant jet crashing straight into the second twin tower and knifing through it, then dark black smoke, terrible bright flames, an unbelieving silence, and finally, slowly, the horrible realization that there had been no pilot error or miscalculation either time, that this was a bold attack, that something brand new and incredibly evil had happened.

Strange sounds gurgled from the back of Danny's throat, sounds like, "No oough" and "Eeeeeeeh." It felt good to let them out.

She rolled off his bed, naked, apparently not sure which private area to shield from his gaze with her long skinny hands. He looked away. Still groggy, she mumbled, "Really gotta pee. Holy Jesus."

Danny sprinted back to the kitchen. The television there was still on and Mr. Cuisinart had finished perking. He winced as another plane crashed into a tower. Weren't there only two twin towers? But it was a replay of what he'd just seen from a slightly different camera angle. "Thank God", he heard himself mumble. He poured two big mugs of coffee, wishing he'd made it even stronger, and hoped she didn't expect cream or sugar. He heard her flush as he entered the bedroom and semi-shouted "There's a robe on a hook behind the door."

She emerged from the john, wearing his green terry robe, a little too long but serving the coverup purpose. They sat apart on the edge of the bed, gulping black coffee, transfixed by the screen. Danny felt a terrible gnawing in the back of his throat. A craving for something from his past. He remembered the bright red Marlboro pack somebody named Linda had left in his car a month ago, remembered how he'd decided to keep it in his dresser on the theory that some date might ask for a smoke after sex and he could be a hero.

"Debbie, would it be..."

"It's Donna, not Debbie." he hadn't heard her snarl before.

"Donna, of course, what was I thinking. I'm so sorry."

"Apology accepted. I wasn't totally sure Danny was right either. Sorry I barked at you."

"Donna, listen, I haven't smoked in two years but I really need a cigarette. I guess I could smoke on the patio if it would bother—"

She cut him off again, but this time her voice was meek, like a scared little girl at the front of the roller coaster line. "Please, may I have one too?"

The Marlboros were in the second drawer, hidden from who knows whom under a bright orange bathing suit. He thought for a moment about where there might be matches, but thinking was hard and the kitchen was near so he lit one cig, then the other from the stovetop burner. She snatched hers from his hand and they took a deep drag in unison, avoiding each other's eyes. He focused on her long fingernails, almost purple but not quite. He wondered whether Revlon sold a nail polish called Almost Purple?

Watching the tragedy was torture, but not watching was out of the question. Strange, almost nonsensical, words poured into the earpieces of the announcers and out their mouths, words like Hamas, Al-Qaeda, Bin Laden, Jihad. David the Brain was on the screen, talking of at least three more possible hijackings. Who the fuck knew what was true and what was rumor?

Passengers were calling spouses and parents from cell phones aboard hijacked planes and even using those incredibly expensive phones mounted on the seatbacks, whispering about Arab men with cardboard cutters and guns and explosives, of flight crews subdued and controls taken by crazed men, of resisters beaten and battered.

Donna looked at her toenails as she said, "Can you imagine what it would be like to be on one of those planes?"

Danny wanted to answer, wanted to tell her imagining was exactly what he was trying to do, imagining the terror, the grief, the impending doom, maybe even the bravery of those poor trapped souls who were simply on their way to a business meeting or a job interview or Disneyland. Instead he said, "No, I can't. How could anybody?"

The cameras shifted back to New York and reports of trapped victims in the towers, on cell phones too, begging for help, choking on smoke, scrambling down endless flights of stairs, struggling for hope and answers in the face of chaos.

Danny felt like he had to say something. He rehearsed several lines in his head, but they sounded wrong, either too flip or too corny. What finally emerged was, "Do you get the impression that anyone has a clue as to how to respond to this?"

As if they had heard him, CNBC switched to a feed of the President, who had been in Florida, courting the voting parents of Sarasota second-graders. In the smart frat-boy voice which usually drove Danny up the wall, George W vowed revenge against the perpetrators of what he called an apparent terrorist attack. The speech lasted maybe a minute before he was whisked off to God knows where on Air Force One.

The reports continued to flow in as Danny and Donna smoked and stared. The ogre Vice President and the gap-toothed Condelezza were apparently together in a bunker somewhere. A plane had crashed into the Pentagon, but footage was not yet available.

Mostly Untrue Stories

And then WHOOSH, right there on the screen, the entire South Tower imploded, like a past-its-prime Vegas hotel. Donna cried, giant sobs rolling up, down and through the green robe. Danny wished he could cry, but his pain was caught up in the tightening in the back of his throat. Her sobbing graduated to wailing. They both kept smoking, lighting each new cylinder off the butt of the consumed one. On the tube, people were running through smoky streets, trying to breathe but not inhale, trying to flee a danger they could not comprehend.

Danny threw his arms around her, feeling the heat of her body through the thick terrycloth, kissing her hot red cheeks, trying in vain to sop up the salty tears that came faster than he could lick them away,

She tried to pull away. "How can you even—"

"Donna, please hold me and stay, just hold and stay, hold and stay. This is not about sex. Please, I need you close."

She started to resist and the words, "I gotta get to work" slipped out before she realized that "hold and stay" was exactly what she needed, too.

One plane was on course to the White House or maybe the CIA headquarters in Langley. Another was in the Midwest. Another was out in Pennsylvania somewhere and heading southeast. And then it crashed outside Pittsburgh in a town impossibly called Shanksville.

Whoever might have remained in the South Tower was silent, but cellphones still called loved ones and Nine-One-One from the North, charting their progress down the stairwells, waiting for the firemen and gas masks the Mayor or the Governor had promised, saying goodbyes just in case.

Danny switched channels, seeking information and reassurance from Tom Brokaw, from Peter Jennings, from Wolf Blitzer. But they seemed as confused, as lost, as scared, as the CNBC gang.

The plane in the Midwest wasn't hijacked after all. Irish and Puerto Rican firemen and cops dashed across the screen but didn't seem to have any sense of where they were headed. Looters wearing ski masks were already on the streets, targeting the discount electronics stores, encountering no resistance. People were jumping off the roof of the North Tower, apparently preferring rapid certain death to terror. Hordes of New Yorkers, rich and poor, were on the bridges on foot and in wheelchairs, seeking the suddenly promised lands of Brooklyn and Staten Island.

And then the North Tower imploded, more efficiently and decisively than the South if that were possible, and the cellphones and their owners all died, and Danny sobbed great sobs into Donna, matching her rhythm sob for sob, as their Marlboros smoldered in the ashtray.

Nowhere to Hide

If I intentionally shorten my strides and start with my back against the bars, I can take six steps before my pecs are flush with the gray back wall of my cell. There's a bed, really more of a cot, and a rusty metal nightstand with one sometimes-stuck drawer. On the nightstand is a dingy old lamp that no longer sports its shade, just a glary 60-watt bulb. When it burns out, I'll likely wait a week or two for a replacement.

In the far left hand corner is a primitive toilet and a tiny sink. I clean them twice a day because it's something to do and I'm scared of disease. My sister visited last week and brought me a bright blue exercise mat. I wash it every day now and do my pushups and sit-ups on it. I keep track of my exercise regimen with my #2 pencil in a spiral notebook which I was allowed to buy at the prison store. I write small in it, not sure whether I'll have a chance to buy another when all the pages are used up. I guess I could erase everything and start over if I had to. It's not like there's anything profound. When my pencil point goes blunt, I wait for a guard in a good mood and ask him for a sharpening.

I do thirty pushups and sixty sit-ups four times a day in my cell. On Tuesday and Thursday afternoons, I get 45 minutes to work out in the gym with four or five other prisoners. They look and act like thugs. Three guards watch us, right hands on their billies, just daring us to make trouble. I don't ever take them up on that dare.

I'm not a thug or a criminal. I'm a state college grad with a degree in business administration. I was fifth in my executive training class at Bank of America. I've written financial plans for couples with net worths in eight figures. I've dated attorneys and doctors and CPA's, most of them damn attractive.

I made one stupid mistake thanks to my so-called buddy Frank Mitchell, who convinced me to down a Jack Daniels shooter after three Dos Equis and then told me I was fine to drive home, only three miles to the condo. And yeah, I was seeing four headlights coming at me from each approaching car, but if I squinted my left eye closed it almost always turned back to two. The radio was turned to an FM oldies station and Jose Feliciano was singing "Light My Fire". And as I was driving, I actually thought why don't I just (a) pull over, and (b) take a nap. And apparently, I did (b) but not (a).

And I think I remember the instant I woke up and saw the woman in the crosswalk pushing the stroller and realized I was going to hit her square on and I know I slammed the brake but it was much too goddamn late and I felt the thud and actually thought about hit and running but that's not my style so I pulled over and dialed 911. The dispatcher said someone had already called it in and then mumbled "drunk driver" and hung up. Next thing I knew they were reading me my rights and cuffing me. I passed out in the back of the police car.

My lawyer advertised on TV. He had silver hair and bushy eyebrows and reminded me of Bob Barker. He told me we could plead to vehicular manslaughter and not risk a conviction for second degree murder which might cost me ten years. He also told me he'd need twenty grand up front if I wanted to go to trial.

I didn't have twenty grand or much of a case so I pled. And my victim's family, disabled husband and five cute clean kids, showed up for the sentencing. The Honorable Martha Bennett, a tiny black-robed woman with a long wrinkly forehead and a beaky nose, rejected the DA's recommendation of sixteen months in a minimum security facility. She decided to make me an example and sent me to this godforsaken joint for three years. She did offer me the option of withdrawing my guilty plea, but one more glance at my victim's family convinced me that was not an avenue I wanted to pursue.

There is nowhere to hide here. I spend a lot of time lying in bed because my body is shielded from view by the thin wool blanket that covers me. I sometimes put the blanket over my head, too. That's against the rules and it'll usually be only a minute or two before the guard barks "Show me your face, Jimmy. Now! You don't want me coming in there."

When I pee, I sit down like a woman because at least then I can cover my crotch with my hands. There's always a light on in the cell, even at night, and the guards like to catch you jerking off and say clever shit like, "Oooh, Jimmy, you make me so hot." Sometimes in falsetto.

I dream a lot, mostly when I'm not sleeping. I dream of closing doors behind me and peering out the window at tall slender eucalyptus trees. I dream of lying in a big tubful of sizzling water with a yellow rubber duckie swimming laps around my naked frame, just like when I was seven. I dream of hitting the brakes in the nick of time, opening the car window, and apologizing to the relieved lady pushing the stroller.

Testing

I'd been standing on line at the Golden Spoon, waiting to order a waffle cone stuffed with winter mint and cappuccino yogurt and garnished with bits of Snickers and Heath Bar and hoping I'd remember to ask for the senior discount. Beethoven's Fifth resonated from my pocket, indicating a call from someone who was not a member of my family. I glanced at the phone number, local but not familiar, flipped the phone open and said hello.

A staccato voice responded, just a little too loud. "Richard, Dr. Bernstein, your urologist. We need to talk about your PSA test results. Is this a good time?"

Two stupid first reactions. First, why do doctors always call you by your given name even though you've told them to use your nickname? Is he just looking at the file? Even so, why wouldn't the file say my name is Rick? That's what I asked him to call me. Second, do I relinquish my place in the yogurt line to continue the conversation?

"Richard, are you there? Can we talk now?"

"Sure, Doctor, just give me a minute." I walked outside and stood in front of the closed beauty supply shop two stores down in the strip mall. "Doctor Bernstein, it's Rick. I can talk now. How high was my PSA?"

"It registered 5.4, not terrible for someone your age, Richard, but high enough that I would strongly recommend further testing. I'd like to do an ultrasonic blah blah blah blah and a prostate biopsy."

Part of me wanted to ask what the blah blah blah blah was, but the other part was busy dealing with the implications of biopsy. Bernstein apparently took my silence as an invitation to proceed and his words got faster and faster as I tried in vain to keep up with him, like that bearded Italian biker trying to stay with Lance Armstrong on a Tour de France breakaway. And why was Lance in my head suddenly?

"It's actually quite a simple procedure, should only take fifteen or twenty minutes, no rush to do it at all, prostate cancer grows incredibly slowly. And by the way, statistically you probably don't have it—77% of these come up benign. But I didn't like how it felt up there, that ridge that I mentioned during the physical exam."

I didn't remember any mention of a ridge, but that's just the kind of thing I would repress.

"My office will call you tomorrow to set the appointment. And they'll also send you detailed instructions and a prescription for antibiotics and by the way you need to take a fleet enema the night before. Bye now."

And he was gone, leaving me to figure out what the hell it meant to maybe have prostate cancer and whether I should return to the yogurt line.

The phone rang again, this time Pachelbel's Canon ringtone. "Hola, Carolina, mi esposa," jumped from my lips, false bravado in spades.

"What'd the urologist say? He called here first and I told him to call your cell."

"PSA is high, but not really high. I can't remember the number. He wants to do a biopsy and something with ultrasound, I think. Says the odds are it's not cancer, but I really don't like this."

Shit, I wanted to be nonchalant and reassuring. "When's the biopsy?"

"He says no rush, prostate cancer is slow growing." As I said this, I could feel the cells multiplying down there.

"Are you okay? Do you want to come home? You sound weird."

"I think I should go to my meeting. There'll be plenty of time for moping. I love you."

"I'll be here. I love you too."

I took a deep breath and walked back to the yogurt store. The line was shorter. Let the avoidance begin. The damn brain kept focusing on the cancer. In the car and at the meeting, I thought of my friend Ben and his prostate cancer, how the operation kept him off the golf course for months, how hard it was for him to walk, how he told me his balls swelled up to the size of grapefruits, but wouldn't show me.

I thought of Steve, who basically went on sabbatical from an insanely busy law practice to deal with his prostate and claimed the experience changed his outlook on life. And Pete, who had some kind of treatment in lieu of surgery and swore by it, and my dental tech's husband who had prostate surgery by robot administered by a Chinese surgeon with an unpronounceable name who I might have to talk with.

But mostly I thought of Carol and what kind of caregiver I could be for her if the same shit that she'd been fighting for two years was now raging inside of me. Would we need to hire someone to take care of us? Was the nightmare scenario so tactfully portrayed by the clean-cut Mormon long-term health care salesman about to happen? On the way home, I turned up the radio and tried to focus on the Laker game, but it just didn't work.

Bernstein's scheduler did call the next day. Three weeks would pass before the biopsy could happen. It seemed too long, like it would be a nightmarish period of waiting and worrying. But it wasn't. I buried myself in sports, exercise, writing, games, gambling and any other pastime I could think of, anything that would shield me from the cancer thoughts. I denied myself nothing and ate and drank too much. Carol tried to begin a "what-if dialogue" a couple of times. I changed the subject.

The invasion day arrived and I trudged into Bernstein's office, successfully enamaed. His humorless, big-haired nurse ushered me to a bathroom, and told me to pee in a cup and then meet her in Room 5. Per her instructions, I stripped "from the waist down," tried to cover my lower body with the flimsy paper gown/towel she supplied, and kept my shoes and socks on, "because it's very cold in here."

Then she took my vitals and made a sour face at the blood pressure reading. "ONE FIFTY-THREE OVER NINETY-FIVE," was her indictment.

All I could respond in defense was, "I guess I've got reason to be a little tense this morning."

She was unimpressed, left me to shiver on the table, and told me Bernstein would be in right away. Ten minutes later, she stuck her head in and said, as if for the first time, "Doctor will be with you shortly." The door closed again before I could request a blanket.

Bernstein finally arrived, his perfectly groomed mustache highlighting a pleasant enough face set on a short, skinny body. He was the grown-up successful version of the last kid chosen for the playground basketball games.

He smiled and said, "Richard, how are you this Monday morning?"

"Doctor, please call me Rick. And could I get a real blanket, it's freezing in here?"

He sent the nurse off to find a blanket while he ceremoniously washed his hands. She sneered and her doughy cheeks reddened as she went blanket-fetching, a task certainly below her station.

The good news was that the biopsy procedure really took only twenty minutes. The bad news was that it was incredibly uncomfortable to have this long probe inserted up there and constantly adjusted and readjusted. The so-called "topical anesthetic" didn't do shit. And then Bernstein began to snip off tiny samples of my prostate and the sound inside me was that of a staple gun triggering and releasing, triggering and releasing, twelve or fourteen times in all. I felt trapped and panicky, and realized this would be only the beginning if my 23% chance of cancer came through.

When he finally told me that he was done and about to remove his weapon, the words that left my tongue were, "Thank you."

"Nobody's ever thanked me for that before."

"I'm thanking you for taking your goddamn sword out."

"Touché." He smiled.

I should have said, "No, tushie."

Bernstein told me it "looked pretty good in there," that there would be blood in my semen, stool and urine for a while, that he'd have the results by the end of the week and would call me. "And, Rick, if you haven't heard from us by Friday morning, please call my office."

He actually called me Rick. Maybe we had bonded.

I went directly to lunch with an old friend, sitting gingerly on my sore ass but otherwise okay. I told him where I'd been just because I had to tell someone other than Carol.

As the physical pain began to subside, the emotional pain intensified. I had my regular dental cleaning and asked the tech how her husband was doing. Once again, she sang the praises of the robot surgeon. I forgot his name as soon as I left her chair.

I decided that no news by Thursday wasn't good news, that a clean report wouldn't have to be reviewed or further analyzed, that I'd know something by now if all was well. I moped around the house.

By 10:30 Friday morning, I could wait no longer. "Urology Office, this is Jessica." Bernstein's receptionist was fresh and perky and anxious to please.

"Sir, please hold and I will check your file and see if your results are in." She returned after several uncomfortable minutes. "Sir, your results are not yet in. It's likely that we won't get them until Monday."

Shit. Shit. Shit.

"So, Jessica, tell me what are your office procedures when the biopsy results do come in?"

"Results go to the doctor right away. If everything is fine, the nurse will call you. If there is a problem, you hear from the doctor."

I could not believe she told me that. Now there would be no surprise once I knew the identity of the caller. Might as well tell them to inform me by email or that text thing I still don't understand.

When Carol got home, I told her I had a plan. "If the doctor calls, I'll tell him I would prefer to speak to the nurse." She laughed.

I sulked.

The weekend seemed longer than usual, but finally it was Monday. I charged my cell phone and prayed for the nurse's call. The phone rang, but it was my son, checking in. I lied and told him I was on the other line and would have to call him back. By 10:20, I could wait no longer and hit the speed dial.

"Urology Office, this is Jessica."

I gave her my name and info and there didn't seem to be a speck of recollection. Maybe there was more than one Jessica there. She asked me to hold, but this time there was Pandora, The Dave Brubeck Quartet playing Take Five. I hummed along and wondered why I didn't listen to jazz anymore. My hand shook. I checked my emails for the umpteenth time that morning, just for something to do.

"Richard, they just came in and I have them right here. The Doctor will call you shortly." And she hung up.

I sat at my desk and stared at the computer screen and my eyes glazed and I said the words, "I've got cancer," out loud four or five times just to hear how it sounded. It sounded ominous. I Googled Dave Brubeck and played the entire Take Five album over and over on my computer, losing myself in the music occasionally, only to slip back into catastrophizing.

I made myself focus on people I knew who had beaten cancer, even my own father. But then I'd lose focus and remember those who didn't make it and how sad everyone was at the memorial.

Four hours later, Bernstein finally called. "Good news, Richard, the specimens were all benign. Next checkup in six months. See you then."

I wept.

Those Damn Lips

Pete could never stop staring at those damn lips of hers. Those lips which had smothered him with love and lust an eternity and a half ago. Those lips which had cursed and damned and ignored him and blamed him for everything bad she'd done to herself and to Katie. Those lips which told him to get the hell out and gave him an hour and a half to pack up his stuff and said he'd be hearing from her lawyer. Those lips which spouted lies and half-truths to the sympathetic mediator when Pete only wanted closure and joint custody and a double shooter of Patron.

Katie held his hand tight as they climbed the front steps of the house that was once his home. She was nine now but still Daddy's Little Girl. He snuck a look at his watch, but she caught him in the act. "We're fine. Seven minutes early I'm guessin. And Mom doesn't get all pissy like she used to anyhow."

"And what kinda language is that, young lady?"

"C'mon, Dad, all the kids say it. Even you do sometimes." And she blushed and showed her dimple and he did the same.

Kristin was in the doorway now and those damn lips were even sort of smiling. "Great, you guys are a few minutes early. Katie, how was your weekend with Dad?"

"So fun, Mommy, we ate sushi and went to the zoo and walked around the Gaslamp after ten and there were so many people dressed up."

Pete tasted bile and felt his biceps tighten. He should've reminded Katie that the late night walk in the Gaslamp was their little secret. He waited for the luscious lips to purse and the lashing and slashing to begin. But Kristin's face registered nothing. Could she not have heard?

Kristin gave Katie a dismissive hug and a pat on the butt. "Hop upstairs and unpack your suitcase, my little bunny. Your Dad and I need to match up our calendars for next week."

It took only two halfhearted, "OhMoms" before she ascended.

Pete pulled out his iPhone and Kristin removed her Android from the pocket of her shortish shorts. He waited for her to begin the scheduling session. She was always the first one to speak. But she just stood there with that wacky Mona Lisa smile on her face, as if he was supposed to say something and she was expecting it would be profound or at least witty. He looked away from the luscious lips and down her torso to those incredible bronze legs, straight out of a Playboy Centerfold. He'd seen them even before he'd seen her face, at the gym almost 12 years ago.

He needed to say something quick to break the spell. "Our daughter is quite a handful, isn't she?" was the best he could come up with, and as he was mouthing it, he heard the schoolmarm in Kristin giving him a failing grade for cleverness. He looked up and her smile was still there with a quizzical upturn of the lips added. She did not respond to his question. She put the Android back in her pocket. It seemed she had an agenda.

"Do you ever miss me?"

He smelled her perfume, Obsession by Calvin Klein, he'd know that fragrance anywhere. He stared off into

Mostly Untrue Stories

space, his best deer in the headlight pose, trying to come up with the right answer. Possibilities jumped into his head and were quickly rejected as too blasé, too pushy or just plain stupid. He settled for the truth.

"I deeply miss the Kristin I knew and loved. I don't miss the Kristin who replaced her and turned my life to shit."

The words felt good coming out, like pus from a raw wound left untended too long. Pete took a half step backward and felt his torso tilt away from her, an experienced prizefighter anticipating an attack. He shouldn't have said "shit", "crap" would have done just fine and would have been less likely to inflame her. He knew he needed to mollify her. He opened his mouth, but she spoke first. Even before he heard the words, he noticed the tone, which wasn't vicious

"I've really been awful to you, haven't I? You hung in there a long time with me. I hated your guts for coddling me, for being kind and gentle and sweet and understanding when what I wanted was anger and rejection and a little bit of truth. What you just said was maybe the truest thing you've ever said to me."

He took one tentative step forward and her head was on his shoulder, hot wet sobs soaking his muscled neck. He peeked up the stairs, hoping Katie wasn't eavesdropping, relieved to see only a boring gray hallway. Kristin backed away a bit and dabbed at her face with a tissue that appeared out of nowhere. Those lips parted once again. The words that came out made him feel like his brain might explode.

"If the old Kristin were back, would Petey be interested in dating her?"

He knew he had to be cautious, remembering failed pre-divorce reconciliations which had lasted for weeks or days or sometimes an hour. He needed to get away. He grasped for words and what came out was "I need to pee really bad" and he ran to the bathroom and locked the door from inside. He didn't turn on the fan because he wanted to make sure that she heard that he was really pissing, not just thinking.

Kristin was a narcotic and he was a junkie. He'd had a hell of a time kicking the habit and here she was offering herself up to him once again. Was this just planting the seed for the next cold turkey? Could it possibly be worth it? Could he ever resist those damn lips? And where did Katie fit in this whole picture?

He forced himself to concentrate, to make a mental list of the pros and cons, to analyze the situation like the crackerjack lawyer he knew he was. Then he flushed the toilet and washed his hands and face with cold water and ran a comb through his hair and felt like he had a plan.

He hummed as he walked toward her and tried to sound unemotional. "I need to know how long the old Kristin is likely to stay around. Would you be willing to go back to couple's therapy?"

Her answer surprised him. "If that's what you want."

He had his rhythm now. "And let's not say anything about this to Katie 'til we get much farther along in the process. We don't want to get her hopes up. Agreed?"

"I'd love to agree but I'd be lying. Katie's my best friend and knows exactly what's going on. Why do you think she's still upstairs in her room?"

His rhythm abandoned him. He felt the urge to pee again.

* * *

Pete arrived at precisely 10:49, fashionably early for their 11 AM couple's therapy with Doctor Levy. He'd asked to speak directly to the doctor before setting the appointment and had explained that he was unwilling to attempt reconciliation unless a professional, an expert in the field, felt there was a real chance at returning to their earlier bliss. Levy had chuckled and said something like, "You lawyers, always seeking certainty and expert opinions," before agreeing to a first session on a trial basis, "which will probably run at least an hour and a half, maybe even two." Pete wondered whether he and Kristin would feel like having lunch together after a marathon session like that. He'd made two different reservations on the chance that they might.

The waiting room was a study in gray, each piece of unmatched furniture distinguished only by the neutrality of its palette. The magazine selection was meager and scholarly, nothing vivid or jarring. The brightest items in the room were the hard candy wrappers, boasting (probably falsely) the freshness of their raspberry and orange and lime centers. A chubby young woman wearing a flowery sundress sat in a rusted wheelchair across from him and averted his gaze. A large black and white clock, the kind he remembered from high school classrooms, clicked the waiting time away.

No Kristin.

The water cooler was the only clue that this might be the 21st century, a shinier more metallic gray with three different buttons marked only by icons he didn't understand. He sensed the fat woman watching him and picked a button, shooting water into a gray cup. It turned out to be the perfect temperature. He wished he'd remembered which button he had used. He pulled out his iPhone and checked his stocks, then checked them again. He fidgeted. Still no Kristin. The big hand clicked toward the twelve. She was cutting it tight. He tried not to look at the clock.

A gentle female voice said "Anna" and the wheelchair creaked its way toward and through the door to the inner sanctum just as the clock ticked to the appointed time. Anna gave him a tentative wave, as if acknowledging they had spent meaningful time together.

Pete wondered if he'd somehow given Kristin the wrong address. He pulled out his phone and speed-dialed her. Four rings and straight to, "Hi, it's Kristin—leave me a message and I'll call you back." He was trying to decide what to say when Dr. Levy appeared, a bronzed, bald, mustached man in his fifties with a great big paunch. He cleared his throat, "Mr. Stephens?"

Pete thrust out his hand and liked the just-strong-enough handshake he received. "Doctor, it looks like Kristin isn't here yet. Why don't you just come back in a couple of minutes and we can start?"

Levy nodded and left. Pete realized that the voicemail was still recording, hung up and dialed again. More voicemail. Had she been in an auto accident? Was she standing him up? Why would she do that when getting back together was her idea? Or maybe she was just trying to hurt him by getting his hopes up? Kristin at her worst was capable of that.

Levy returned at ten past eleven. Pete twitched and said, "I don't know what to say."

The doctor said, "C'mon in, you might as well use up the time." Pete noticed that he wore tasseled loafers.

How does one do couples counseling alone?

***

Levy led and Pete followed. Levy's ass was too big for his khakis and Pete had to force his eyes higher because it didn't seem right to stare at his shrink's butt. Levy collapsed into the weathered leather easy chair as if the twenty second hike had exhausted him and motioned Pete toward the over-pillowed couch. Pete wondered how the doctor might react if he assumed the fetal position. Instead he sat and just fidgeted because it seemed weak to apologize for Kristin's no-show.

Levy smiled a gentle father's smile. After a brief millisecond or two of eye contact, he gazed toward the chipped ceiling and asked, "Tell me three things I should know about Kristin."

Pete's hands went to his face, the index and middle fingers of each hand touching the eyelids, the pinky and ring fingers softly caressing the sinuses, the thumbs on the jawbones—his thinking position.

There were so many things about Kristin. How could he pick just three? And what would those choices reveal about himself? He cleared his throat as a preface but no words came out. Then he craned his neck toward the ceiling (and would have stared at its decay if his fingers weren't still covering his eyes) and said, as if summarizing an argument to a judge, "One she's gorgeous, two … um she had an awful childhood, and three she's convinced men will always treat her badly." And he removed his hands from his face and looked past Levy at the fancy framed diplomas on the plaster wall behind his desk.

A door slammed from not too far away. Levy coughed, then said "I'm guessing that's your Kristin announcing her tardy arrival. Why don't you go get her?"

Pete resisted the impulse to say, "Don't tell her what I just said," and returned to the waiting room, not sure whether he wanted to find Kristin there.

Her perfect face was marred with tears and she stood and hugged him, and her smeared makeup migrated from her face to his, and she wept and said, "I'm such a fuckup. Can you ever forgive me?"

And he already had without even knowing why she was late.

It Was So Dark

She took little tiny shuffle steps, feeling with the delicate heel of her pump for the expected cracks in the pavement. She wasn't drunk but now regretted the second glass of Sauvignon Blanc and particularly the time it had taken to consume it. Friday Happy Hour at Friday's had lasted too long and now it was pitch black and this street and the next had no streetlights.

She was only a quarter-mile from home but felt like maybe tonight was the night something bad was going to happen, the night her nightmares just might come true. Her left heel stuck in a crack just for an instant but she was able to right her listing ship. She permitted herself a smile for a second, an attaboy for the feat of dexterity that kept her upright.

It wasn't cold for an early November night, but she was glad for the long black coat she'd worn to work and checked at the bar. Her coat check number had been 23 and she knew that was Michael Jordan's uniform number and thought maybe that was a good omen, but she certainly hadn't met anybody tonight worthy of her time and energy, nobody remotely resembling a superstar.

She sneezed and stumbled the next instant and she heard the throaty "gezundheit" before she felt the hand on her calf, somehow under her coat. The heavy leather purse was her only weapon and she swung it hard, harder than she'd thought she could, in the general direction of the "gezundheit" and shrieked, "Get the hell away from me."

She heard a thud and swung the purse again, and maybe she was just imagining it but she was sure she felt the contact through the purse strap. She wanted to run but running wasn't an option with heels on this sidewalk.

The hand grabbed again for her ankle but it was limper now. She swung the purse a third time, feeling the weight shift to her right foot on the backswing and then the transfer and the follow-through and the satisfying crunch of club meeting ball with the clubface square, but it wasn't a golf club at all, she now remembered, it was a purse and she was swinging at some Gezundheiter who had made the mistake of touching her leg a moment ago.

She felt the sharp impact and heard a thud and then an awful gargle and the limp slimy hand was gone from her leg and there was a faint stench of shit in the air and silence, black as the sky. An owl hooted in the distance, just loud enough to break her trance.

Cell phone, she thought. *I've gotta cell phone in my purse-weapon and I can call 911.*

She unzipped the purse and found the phone by feel, stepping a yard or so away from the interloper as she did so. The phone gave off a little bit of reflected light and she aimed it across the path. The first thing she saw was blood, lots of blood—on the sidewalk. She moved the beam of light a little further and she spotted her assailant, a skinny freckly waif of a child who maybe weighed seventy pounds, dressed in now-bloody rags—and he wasn't goddamn moving one bit.

Alice

The invitation had been scotch-taped to my grey metal locker on the last day of school. Purple ink sprawled out "Ricky" in giant fancy letters on a soft white envelope. There seemed to be curlicues in every letter, including the dot of the i. I'd immediately known to play it cool, that the poster of this note and one or more of her cohorts could be lurking just around the corner or behind one of the marble pillars that had kept Wilson School standing for over half a century. I'd made it a point to scratch under my chin, hinting to whomever might be observing that I was interested in and perhaps a little puzzled by the unexpected correspondence. Then I stuffed the envelope into my pocket, to be opened in a more private place.

I met up with Frankie and Sid outside the front door. We almost always walked home from school together and were best friends, but there was heaviness in the air that day that wasn't a result of the humidity. Nobody wanted to speak first. Then I saw the corner of a creamy envelope sticking out of Sid's khaki pocket and, without even thinking of Frankie, said "Didja open the envelope? Whattazit say?"

Sid looked panicked, like he'd been caught with a finger in the frosting, and Frankie smiled with relief and said, "I was wondering whether you meatheads got one too." It turned out none of us had opened them yet and we decided to run all the way to Frankie's and check them out together. Their legs were a lot longer than mine, but I kept up. The adrenaline was definitely flowing. We'd just learned about adrenaline in science class.

Frankie's parents had a live-in maid named Lucille who looked like the picture of Aunt Jemima on the maple syrup bottle. Lucille greeted us by name (I was always Mistah Ricky) and had large glasses of milk and still-warm chocolate chip cookies waiting for us. I loved Lucille's cookies and the way they dissolved into the river of milk and flowed southward into my gullet and beyond.

Lucille was not happy when we took the milk and cookies upstairs to Frankie's room, but Frankie mumbled something about privacy and promised to bring back the empty glasses and Lucille went back to her easy chair and Life Magazine.

We sat on the tan carpeted floor of Frankie's oversize room, almost as big as the master bedroom at my house, and placed the three envelopes at the center of our triangle. I closed my eyes while Frank shuffled them and then I picked numbers one, two and three in order. Sid got to open his first as we gaped. The invitation was in that same purple ink, printed not script but still oozing curlicues. It invited us to a "small gathering to celebrate our graduation from sixth grade" the next Wednesday at Cookie Goldman's house from 7 to 10 PM. It told us that "Sweets (ha ha) and punch would be served." And it advised us that it was "imperative to RSVP right away by calling Cookie or her Mother at RO6-4377." As I write this now, I keep wanting to insert an area code, but there was no such thing then. It was signed "The Girls."

All three invitations said the same thing, but they were clearly written by different hands sharing the same inkwell. Mine had the most curlicues, which made me feel important. We examined each invite, looking for hidden clues. This party felt different.

Frankie wanted to know what a gathering was. I ventured that it might be less formal than a party or maybe just smaller. Sid smiled and called me naive, then suggested that gathering might be a code word for "make out party." As further evidence, he cited the use of "ha ha" and the need to rsvp. I felt a tingle but told him he was dreaming. Those parties didn't happen till you got to junior high.

Sid and Frankie spoke at the same time. "So, are we going?"

We agreed we were and drew straws as to who would call to RSVP. I drew the short one and dialed the number. Cookie answered. Nobody ever understood why she was called Cookie. Her real name was Judy and she was scrawny with a Brooklyn accent. "Cookie, this is Ricky and I am calling to accept the invite to the, uh, gathering. And Frankie and Sid are coming too."

"Frankie's coming?", she swooned, then righted herself and said, as if her mother might be beside her,

"Thank you so much for calling so promptly. We'll see you boys then."

I'd convinced my Mom that I needed a haircut right away, before I went away to camp, and she reluctantly agreed even though haircuts were cheaper at camp. I'd told Sal the barber, one of the few grownups I was allowed to address on a first-name basis, that I wanted a flat-top, almost like the tough kids wore, but not quite. And I'd purchased a brand new tube of Sal's finest crew cut wax to force those sides up. My black chinos had been starched a little and the crease seemed sharp as a pen-knife. I'd started with only a new white t-shirt on the top, sleeves rolled up to reveal what I thought were pretty impressive biceps, but my Mom drew a line in the sand there and told me a collared shirt was a must. I finally opted for a blue striped button down, but I wasn't happy with it. The white t shirt was still underneath and might make an appearance once the gathering got going.

We were a good ten minutes late for the party because Sid's mom insisted on taking pictures of the three of us, dressed to kill. She sipped her white wine and giggled out

"You guys've got enough grease on your hair to fry a dozen chickens, I'll bet." She always made it a point to hug me goodbye, engulfing my little frame in her soft warmth, and her hug that night was extra-firm and longer. I was impatient to get to the party, but not impatient enough to offer much resistance.

When we left his house, Sid apologized for his mother, but Frankie and I both said it was fine and Frankie even said, "You're supposed to be fashionably late for parties—that's what my Mom always tells my Dad."

I rang the doorbell and heard giggles on the other side. Cookie answered, dressed in a silky royal blue dress and nylons which showed off surprisingly shapely legs. She was shaking her index finger at us and saying "You naughty boys are late. You had us worried." I thought about explaining about Sid's mother, but didn't have a chance. Alice Bader stepped in front of Cookie and held her hand out to me. When I didn't respond fast enough, she took my hand in hers and led me over the doorstep and into the house. "You're with me tonight, Ricky', she cooed, "I hope that's OK." And she squeezed my meaty fingers with her delicate ones and I felt a wave of syrupy stuff flow through my innards and mumbled something profound like "That's cool."

This was not an Alice Bader I'd ever seen before. She was always shy and bookish at school, with frizzy mousy-brown hair, a khaki-like complexion that never smiled, and maybe just a hint of facial hair around the muzzle. She generally dressed in long smock-like dresses, miniature versions of what the women of the Wild West wore. But not that night. She wore a sleek green dress with matching high heels. The dress had a little collar and was open enough to reveal the primitive beginnings of cleavage. I immediately wondered what I had been programmed to wonder, whether there were "falsies" involved. I didn't really know what a falsie was or how I would spot it, but I knew enough to wonder.

The bottom of Alice's dress revealed plenty of leg encased in beige nylons with a dark seam down the back. The nylons were likely tied to a garter belt or maybe even a girdle, yes probably a girdle I thought as I took a little inobtrusive peek at her ass, but maybe my glance wasn't that little or inobtrusive because she caught me looking and said "What are you looking at?" and I smiled and said "You look very pretty tonight, Alice" and she said "You are such a cutie" and squeezed my hand and led me toward the sounds of music emanating from the basement, the Jackie Gleason Orchestra oozing out the ballad My Funny Valentine.

Alice led the way down the narrow stairway to the finished basement, keeping hold of my hand while her other hand used the railing for balance. I didn't want to let go either. The room was dark, the only lighting from a small candle with a piney scent and the red ON button of a Zenith record player stacked with hours and hours worth of LP records. There were three other couples on the three large couches which formed three quarters of a circle in the center of the room. I could recognize some of the occupants, but not others. It kinda depended on how close they were to the candle. There were a couple of grunts of "Hiya Ricky" to which I grunted back. Alice led me toward the unoccupied side of a couch far from the candle and motioned for me to sit. "I think I got us the best spot, don't you?" I knew how to answer that question and said "You sure did." She giggled and said "Flatterer", but it wasn't an accusation of anything wrong. The basement smelled like a cross between a department store and a locker room. The air was thicker than it should have been.

I banged my knee on the coffee table and grunted, "Crap."

Two couched classmates said, "Ssshh."

I turned to Alice and asked in what I thought was a moderate tone, "So Alice, what are you going to do this summer?"

Four couched classmates said, "Shussssh" in unison.

Alice whispered, "We can talk later," and sealed my lips shut with a tiny close-mouthed kiss. I didn't speak again for almost an hour.

Alice curled her legs under her on the couch and lowered her head softly onto my chest. She guided my right hand to her shoulder and planted a soft semi-juicy kiss on my neck. I rubbed her shoulder a little and she sighed. I moved my hand a couple of inches down toward her chest. She let it rest for just a second and then took my hand firmly in hers and moved it back to the shoulder. There were apparently rules to be followed here. She taught me what was acceptable and what was not. I wanted so badly to touch a perky breast but I was afraid it would break the spell. We hugged and kissed for what seemed like hours, but turned out to be about forty minutes. The victrola played instrumental ballad after ballad, slow songs featuring syrupy trombones and flutes. I sang the lyrics in my head and I'm sure Alice did too.

"Five minutes till cake and punch." Cookie had broken the communal mood. Alice reacted immediately, freezing in what I thought was mid-kiss and pulling away. She kicked her legs out from under her, put her shoes back on and stood up. I felt a twinge of rejection till I saw the same scene unfolding with the six other couples. The girls were all straightening their wrinkled clothing and trudging toward the stairs like the lemmings I'd read about in a science book.

The cake and punch were served upstairs. The dining room table had been extended to its fullest and covered with a red white and blue paper tablecloth. There were plastic forks in the exact color of Cookie's dress (I knew this because I overheard the girls yakking about it) and napkins that matched the tablecloth. The cake was gooey and gummy and had lots of whipped cream flowers. The punch was pink and sweet. It wasn't good, but it made you thirsty so you kept drinking it.

The girls had all "freshened up," but the guys looked disheveled, hair jutting out at odd angles, shirts only halfway tucked in, lipstick smears on most faces and a few ears. We sat around the table and the girls talked girl talk and the guys said nothing and squirmed in their seats and ate their cake and drank lots of punch. Cookie's parents tried to get the guys engaged, but quit after five straight questions were answered with a single word and a droop of the head. We were relieved when Mrs. Goldman said, "Why don't you kids go back downstairs and Daddy and I will clean up."

I thought about using the bathroom, but it would have been embarrassing to ask where it was so I raced downstairs with the rest of the guys and we waited for our companions to re-engage. Alice was the first of the ladies to return and we immediately picked up right where we left off. There was a tiny morsel of whipped cream flower almost the exact color of her lipstick at the corner of her mouth and I tasted it and said, "Sweet" without thinking.

She said, "You're so adorable" and planted the wettest kiss yet on my increasingly-chapped lips. The saxophones played *I Only Have Eyes For You* and I sang the words softly to her eyelids and she snuggled in even closer.

The reverie broke with Mrs. Goldman's, "Five minutes 'til the party's over," emanating from the top of the stairs.

The girls began the disengagement process, but there was more resistance this time. We all knew that there would not be an Act 3 and what awaited us was a long walk home. But somebody got to the light switch and flipped it and the spell was broken, each of us shrinking away from our partner for fear of God knows what ridicule. We did walk up the stairs in couples, hand in hand, but the hands were dropped and distances established as soon as we reached the main floor.

Alice reached into her pocketbook and pulled out a shred of paper with her camp address and a big heart with an arrow drawn through it. "Write me and I'll write back, I promise," she whispered wetly into my ear, and the next thing I knew I was out the door with Frankie and Sid.

We walked maybe a block or two in silence and then Sid and I said at exactly the same time, "That was kinda cool," and Frankie just smiled his big wide grin and said, "Yeah."

I crept out of bed early the next morning, feeling sticky and confused, and took a shower way before I usually would have. By the time I strolled down to the breakfast table, Dad was long-gone and my little brother had oatmeal all over his face. Mom had her June Cleaver personality turned on. "Well aren't you nice and clean already, my big boy. How'd it go last night?"

I tried to eliminate the squeak from my voice and replace it with basso nonchalance. "Okay, I guess."

And then Frankie walked right through the side door and into the kitchen and started singing in his most whiney singsong, "Ricky's got a girlfriend. Ricky's got a girlfriend. Ricky's got a girlfriend. And Alice is her name."

June Cleaver batted her eyes and looked perplexed. "Honey, who is this Alice?"

My little brother's beady eyes were all of a sudden red, "Yeah. who is this Alice?"

I glared at Frankie, whose arms were crossed over his chest. "Just a girl I know who was at the party last night. And Frankie was with Cookie Goldman." I thought this might end it but I was mistaken.

Frankie could look very self-righteous when he put his mind to it. "Well, Mrs. S, Ricky is certainly correct that I spent some time with Cookie last night, but we've long agreed that we are good friends only, kinda brother and sister. Ricky and Alice Bader, on the other hand, are head over heels."

I wanted to fight back, but couldn't figure out how. I knew I'd be punished if I uttered the curse word 'bullcrap' and I couldn't think of anything else to say. Tears welled up. I raced from the table up the stairs to my room, shouting, "Don't believe him, don't believe him," over and over, realizing they'd be crazy not to believe Frankie.

I moped around for the rest of the day and Mom left me alone. My trunk was packed for camp and I left the following day, my brother in tow. He asked me about Alice once, just before we got on the bus, and I twisted his arm behind his back and told him I might have to break it off if he ever mentioned her again. He got the message.

Alice sent me 13 letters that summer and I responded to each one. Hers were long rambling letters written in a beautiful flowing hand in purple or green or crimson ink. They were mostly narratives about her life at camp, not very different from the letters I expected she wrote to her parents, with stories about Color War competitions, a measles outbreak, tasteless food, a canoe trip where the sleeping bags got soaked. But in each of her letters, tucked between the newsy nuggets, there'd be a teaser like, "Hope your sweet lips are missing mine," or "Still thinking about you in Cookie's basement," and I'd feel the pull in my groin that my camp tried to minimize with saltpeter and fantasize about the rest of my life with Alice and how happy we would be.

My parents picked us up at camp and we took a little vacation so it wasn't till Labor Day weekend that I was back home. I thought about calling Alice that weekend, looked for times when my house was deserted and I'd have unfettered phone access and privacy. There were two such times and at both I froze and chickened out. What if her father answered? If he was taking a message, would he force me to spell my last name? What if nobody answered? Would I try again or just deem it a sign? Could their family be away for the weekend? Maybe Cookie would know—should I call her? If I did, what would I say if HER father answered? It would be so much easier if Alice called me. Maybe she had and there was no answer.

In the end, I did nothing but mope around and wait for school to start. I'd never before debated with myself about which shirt and socks to wear to class, but that was a major part of how I spent that long weekend. The fireworks were blasting away overhead when I decided on the long-sleeved blue-striped oxford shirt even though Tuesday was scheduled to be eighty degrees plus. I remember actually debating whether my bare arms were a positive or negative characteristic.

All the seventh graders in town were assigned to Clinton School that fall so it was a new experience for everybody. Sid, Frankie and I stood in the playground, backs against the netless arched iron soccer goal, surveying our classmates as they arrived in ones and twos and threes. Frankie broke the silence. "Who the hell are all these people? We don't know anybody anymore?"

Sid and I nodded our heads in agreement. Then Frankie said, "There's your Alice" and I saw her walking through the gate with a tall girl I'd never seen before and she was wearing a shortish tan skirt which really showed off her sunburned legs and her hair was in a ponytail and I waived and she looked up and saw me and our eyes met for just a fraction of a second and then she shrugged her shoulders and turned away and I knew whatever we had was over and I didn't know why. I mumbled "potty break" and left my friends for the privacy of a tiny grey-tiled bathroom stall with a broken lock where I held my head in my hands and wondered how I'd screwed up.

Alice and I never spoke again though we occasionally nodded. We were in classes together and had mutual friends. I think somebody once mentioned that there was another guy, older and taller, who she'd met at camp. I didn't want to know that much, and certainly not any more.

Three weeks into the school year, I burned her letters one by one at night on the vacant lot on the corner near Dr. Drabkin's house. It probably looked to the world like some kid sneaking a smoke. That's if you assume the world was actually looking.

There's a part of me deep inside that's never gotten over the loss of Alice. Maybe once a year I feel the same lump-in-the-throat sadness I felt sitting on that bathroom stall when I'm being rejected unexpectedly. Maybe I hear that a treasured client has brought his new business to another lawyer. Or an old friend doesn't return my calls. Or one of my kids forgets my birthday. And in every one of those cases, I grieve a little and don't try to find out the reason for the rejection.

On the airplane on the way to my twentieth high school reunion, I decided it was time to speak with Alice, to find out what had really happened to justify her turning away, to know whether it was about her or about me. I arrived at the festivities, looking tan and fit, and was presented with the updated class yearbook. I went directly to her page. There was Alice's graduation picture with only the word "deceased" below it.

Hit the Button

I'm not really nervous about this surgery. Yeah, it's a spinal fusion, a bigger deal than the reaming they did last time, but I'll be out cold, having a wonderful snooze. I'll awaken to soreness but the pain in my hamstring will be gone. The specially fitted brace will be a little intimidating, but it's only to protect me against my wife Karen driving the car into a ditch, or something like that. Karen kisses me and they roll me away into four hours of oblivion.

"You're finally awake now. How do you feel?" This from a bold and unfamiliar voice. I feel invaded, like she awakened me from a deep sleep simply to bolster her ego. Then I open my eyes and see the recovery room nurse, steely chin but compassionate eyes, and sense she is my friend, my rock. I open my mouth to tell her I am alive and ok, but no words come out, only a little drool. She giggles. She's certainly seen this before.

"Robert, you are still very woozy, but you need to listen to me for just a second."

Is she about to tell me the operation didn't work?

"Robert, this blue button here is your pain medicine. Whenever you want you can have a shot of morphine, which will take away your pain."

I had a button for my operation two years ago and never used it. The pain was never that bad.

"Now show me you understand me by hitting the button and I'll leave you to your snoozing for a while longer."

I don't really feel any pain but hit the button anyway.

"Great," she says and pats my sweaty brow.

I wake again and Karen is there, looking tired and scared. My hand is still on the painkiller button. My mouth is very dry. From deep in my throat, two words begin their journey, losing momentum as they go, but still emerging from my chafed thin lips, "Ice chips."

I'd watched Karen awaken over the last forty years in too many recovery rooms and seen her eyes sparkle with rapture as I plastic-spooned tiny ice chips into her mouth.

Now I finally understand. I want that icy-wet coolness in my mouth so bad I can feel it in my balls. Karen looks toward the nurse and the nurse apparently says yes. One tiny chip slips past the teeth and I instantly, urgently want another. I give the "C'mon, c'mon" gesture with my right hand. I don't want to be patient. I hit the button by accident. I'm aware of two more ice chip raptures before I return to delirium.

I'm awake again and I guess I'm in my room now. Karen is sitting next to the bed, her wig a little askew, her freckly face lacking its usual glow. She's just begun a chemo vacation, but you wouldn't know it from the glazed look in her eyes. I know it has been a very long day for her. I open my mouth and like magic there is an ice chip on my tongue. What a woman I married! I pucker my lips in the kiss shape and then immediately open them, just in time for the next cold morsel.

I am really loopy, having difficulty staying attuned and awake. Friends come to visit and shake their heads as they leave, apparently disappointed that I'm unable to appreciate their gesture visit or to converse in anything resembling English. My duty nurse is a sturdy woman who reminds me of my secretary Maureen. She encourages me to hit the button whenever I need to.

Karen whispers in my ear. "Honey, I need to go home and take a nap, is that okay? Here's one more big ice chip, I'll call you later."

I hit the button.

It's hard to know whether I'm awake or dreaming. I'm Richie Cunningham at dinner with the family on Happy Days, lying to my parents about the math test I have tomorrow, eating pot roast and mashed potatoes and just-defrosted corn off the cob. It's quiet and peaceful and delightfully boring till I hear that strident voice, the voice of the Fonz.

"Okay, Mike, now what ya gotta understand is that my goal as your nurse is ta keep ya as free from pain as I know how. I've got a, how shall I say it, special relationship, with the duty nurse in charge of the drugs."

I open my eyes and see the guy, wearing scrubs, and he does look like Fonzie, thick eyelashes and brows and that wicked smile of somebody who's absolutely sure he knows how to beat the system.

"Ever use twenny milligrams of Ambien, Mike? No, well that's what's gonna keep you asleep through tonight, that and the morphine I'll shoot into ya whenever you wake up and tell me you hurt. And lemme tell ya right now, if there's any doubt, you're gonna tell me ya hurt."

The divider curtain blocks my view of my roomie, whose name apparently is Mike. Mike wails a horrible guttural sound.

"Mike, I think you just told me your leg is hurtin'. I got the needle right here. Old Tony's gonna kill the pain for ya right now, right now."

I hear a sigh and a very small voice saying, "Thanks Tony." Hard to believe it's the same voice that just wailed. I hit the button.

Now I'm in Chicago and having dinner at Morton's or someplace like Morton's with my old buddy John Simonson. We're wearing our three-piece wool suits like lawyers used to do all the time and not just in court and we're eating giant wads of rare beef and drinking lots of deep red Cabernet and getting shitfaced. We bemoan the fact that neither of us drinks to this kind of excess anymore and we decide to have a contest, right there at Morton's, to see who can piss all over themselves better. "Just let it go, you'll love it," he says, and I do. My medium gray pinstriped slacks are soaking wet and I don't give a crap. It is so incredibly liberating.

"Open your eyes, Mr. Greenberg, time to take your vitals." I pry my lids open and she looks incredibly like I expected her to, chubby, dimple-cheeked, a blond who probably played trombone in the University of Nebraska Marching Band. Her nametag says she's MarthaMae. She sticks something in my ear and something on my arm and begins spouting numbers which have no meaning to me.

It's hard to figure out what I want to say and harder still to mouth the words. Eventually, they mumble out. "Wet ... down ... there."

She pulls the covers away. I shiver. "Sir, you've pulled your catheter out. I'll get your RN. Wait here."

Where did she think I might be going? And why the hell didn't she cover me back up. Is she punishing me? My shivers triple.

She returns with a skinny brunette with braces on her teeth. She's got that schoolmarm arch in her back. "Mister, you cannot be permitted to pull out your catheter. It is dangerous and also very messy and we nurses simply have too much to do. Now why would you do a thing like that?"

I force myself to focus on the answer. "Well, I'm in this contest with John to see who can piss on himself better and I guess it must have gotten in the way..."

A light goes on in her sinewed olive-skinned face. "Sir, may I ask where you think you are?"

A trick question? I look at her in her scrubs and me hooked up to the IV and realize I'm not at Morton's anymore. I smile. I know the answer. "I'm in the hospital."

"Good, and where is the hospital?"

This one is a slam-dunk. "Chicago."

"What?"

"Chicago, but I don't know which street."

She turns to the fat trombone player. "MarthaMae, clean him up and change the sheets while I go get a new catheter."

I hit the button and soon I'm back at Morton's swapping stories with John. The table is cleared but now we are drinking 50-year-old port from little tiny crystal glasses until John says this is bullshit and we get big pinot glasses full of port so we can piss better and it's working and we're laughing and pissing and John lets out this great big fart in our plush banquette and I'm laughing and—

"Mr. Greenberg, you pulled out your catheter again. I'm going to get Tina."

Tina stands over me, forcing herself to take deep breaths. A nerve in her right cheek keeps twitching. After five or six big exhales, she says, far too loud, "And where are we now?"

She seems like such an unhappy person. I'm glad I have the right answer. "In a hospital in Chicago."

But I get no congratulation, no gold star from the teacher. She looks furious, but determined to control her anger. She turns to MarthaMae, somehow convinced that I won't be able to hear what she says next. "Why do I get these nutcases? I'll clean him up. You go find one of those condom catheters. If I put it on tight enough, he won't be able to rip it off."

She's not as gentle as MarthaMae was. I hit the button.

"Wake up, sir, and where are we this morning?" I don't have to open my eyes to know that it is MarthaMae, but I do. The clock says 6:15. I guess Karen never returned.

"Scripps Memorial Hospital, La Jolla, do I get a star?"

God, is she relieved. "Yes, you do. And Tina will be so pleased too. Everything feel okay this morning, Mr. Greenberg?"

"Can you please check my right bedstocking. It feels twisted and is cutting into my leg. Maybe you could even take the stocking off?"

She flips the covers off and I start shivering. She touches the right leg. It's tender as hell. "The stocking is fine and pain this early is typical. If it hurts, hit the button." She leaves.

"I wish I had a morphine button, I'd be hitting it every waking minute." It's my roomie Mike. We're still separated by a curtain divider that neither of us can get out of bed to open.

I ask through the divider, "What happened to you?"

"Guys' trip to Thailand. Racked up my leg on a motorcycle. It's all fucked up. I might lose it."

Before I can figure out how to respond, he gasps and screams into the microphone, "Tony, bring a needle quick."

And I hit the button.

I'm awakened by the rattle of carts and silverware and dishes. "Señor, I bring you breakfast. And you need to fill out these menus, por favor." There's a tray in front of me with too many unattractive choices. I pick at the top of an over-honeyed bran muffin and contemplate the lunch and dinner choices. Nothing sounds good.

I wonder when they last painted this room. I still can't see Mike, but I see his visitor. They're doing guy talk, analyzing pro football and Duke basketball and how many tournaments Tiger will win this year. I'm not sure what the semi-private room etiquette is supposed to be. Am I invited to participate or should I actively ignore them, pretend they are not there, not dilute Mike's experience with his guest? I know I'd share Karen with Mike. I wouldn't have a choice. She'd want to know all about him and his injury and wouldn't be hesitant to start up the conversation, to ask whether he'd like a cookie or some trail mix or a pillow or an iced tea. I'm reminded of the woman who gave Karen an ultimate compliment when she said, "You are so very inclusive."

I'm spared the call on whether to join the conversation by the visitor himself. His chair is facing me. He's tall and skinny and has a buzzcut. "Hey, don't I know you? I'm Steve Kelly." He thrusts his hand out instinctively, then pulls it back like maybe he shouldn't be touching just anybody in a hospital.

He does look familiar, but the name means nothing. My mouth is wide open to indicate I'm thinking, trying to find the missing link, but it hurts my brain.

His brain works better. "San Diego Athletic Club. Noontimes and you used to sweat like crazy on the stair-stepper and watch Chicago Cubs baseball games with your buddy McCarthy on the bike. Am I right?"

He's right on and I tell him so. I introduce myself and Steve opens the curtain that has separated Mike from me since I moved in. Mike has curly receding surfer hair, tired Irish eyes, only a hint of a scraggly beard after many days without a shave. I'm invited to give my opinion on whether to take the Patriots and give the fourteen points. The muffin tastes better and I wonder why my tray included milk, tea, orange juice, and apple juice but no coffee.

Steve prods Mike into telling the story of his accident.

Mike's eyes brighten. "So, there's five of us fifty-somethings on this guys trip to Southeast Asia and we land in Bangkok and fly to Phuket where the tsunamis hit a couple of years ago."

His leg sits above the covers and I don't want to look at it, bandages or not. How can this guy be so mellow, so one of the boys, when he may be losing a leg?

"And so, this big blue diesel truck takes us and five smelly diesel motorcycles on a long slow drive to Asia fucking-nowhere and there's this giant dirt hill and we're supposed to ride to the top and it's not a race but nobody wants to be last so we hightail it up and it's high enough so you can actually see the ocean from the top, which is very cool."

He pauses for a breath. Calypso music plays. It's my cellphone ring and it's Karen. Mike's nod tells me he'll put his story on hold while I answer the call. I tell Karen I'm ok. She says she'll shower and see me at the hospital in about an hour. I sense relief in her voice, like maybe she wasn't sure after yesterday that I'd ever be capable of having a rational conversation.

I put the phone back on the tray and eat a fat muffin crumb. "Sorry for the interruption, Mike. Please go ahead."

"And so now I realize that the dangerous part of this adventure is getting down the hill and all of a sudden, I'm feeling very chicken as the other guys start plowing down like Robert Redford in Downhill Racer. And I eat my pride and decide I'm walking the bike down and hold onto the handlebars and start pushing it. And ... and ... and ... remember how with the old VW Bugs you could jump start them by pushing them? Well that's what this motherfucking yellow bike does."

And in a flash, he's turned from animated to agitated. His right hand balls into a fist and he's slamming it down onto the extra pillow, like doing that will make the hard part of the story easier to tell.

"And I hold on for dear life and then I feel the worst pain of my life and I look down and God, God it was awful to see, the gore, the mangled bones sticking out, all that blood

Mostly Untrue Stories

and I'm still holding on to the bike like that's the right thing to do."

I'm conscious of my own right leg and how incredible tender it feels, way under the covers a million miles from Thailand. I reach for the button, then decide to tough it out.

The rest of Mike's story is a tale of third world blundering, non-equipped so-called ambulances, lifeline helicopters without fuel, morphine supplies drained, unsterile IVs. The cadence of his fist-pounding slows.

"The medical treatment got much better when the guys got me back to Bangkok, but I decided to get home right away. The US Consul was a big help, the flight was hell, and here I am in Scripps Hospital just about three days after the incident."

I can't believe he can call it *the incident*.

There's a strange silence in the room now. I want to ask him what's next, what do the doctors say, but I feel like an interloper, that I don't know him well enough to be entitled to ask.

The silence ends when Steve does the asking. "So, what's next, Mikey?" Mike's a wee bit vague. "I saw a doctor yesterday. Nice guy but standoffish. Can't remember his name, but it starts with a B. He said the next 24 hours or so will be critical to whether I get to keep the leg."

That does it. I hit the button.

Nobody's sure what to say next. Fortunately, Mike has a new visitor. She bustles in and takes charge. She's blond and cute with heavy hips and thighs. She's laden with shopping bags. Mike introduces her as his ex-wife and close friend Suzie. Suzie tries to close the curtain, but Mike tells her to leave it open, that "Bob's a good guy, like family." Suzie shakes her head and I wonder whether their marriage broke down because Mike spent too much time with guy-friends who were "like family". But she doesn't close the curtain. She asks me what I'm in for and I feel like I need to apologize because it was only a back operation. I doze off.

I awaken as a tiny shriveled eighty-year-old woman in a pink velour sweat suit walks into the room with her perfectly groomed French poodle. "Robert," she squeaks, "I'd like you to meet Fluffy. I can put her up on the bed with you? She's very affectionate."

Can I be hallucinating? A dog in the hospital? I wave her off and she is obviously miffed. She's all too real.

"Fluffy just wants to make nice. Let Fluffy come give you a big juicy kiss."

"Please, go away."

"OK, but Fluffy and I will be back tomorrow. You'll love it when she licks your face."

I want to hit the button again, but I don't. I drift off to sleep anyhow. I dream of amputations and prosthetics, of my old buddy Tim who still plays great golf on his artificial leg, of the reckless wheelchair basketball players on TV, of my own leg rotting away under the covers in its thigh-high anti-embolism stocking. I awaken to Karen's voice, but she's not talking to me. The curtain is closed and she's on Mike's side of it. Lord knows how long she's been here but it sounds like Karen has fully bonded with Suzie and is already in strategy-planning mode.

"What do you mean, you don't know who the doctor is. Let's get hold of Mike's chart. I'm pretty good at reading those things. I don't care if it's Saturday, we've got to figure out what's going on. And what do the nurses say?"

Suzie sounds resigned to the system. "Not a lot that helps me. That their job is to minimize his pain and that I need to talk to the doctor."

Karen is energized now, ready to step in where the meek fear to tread. And I'm feeling somehow neglected behind my curtain, with a right leg that feels like it's spent the last few hours in a cactus patch. But I'm sure I'll be fine and I don't want to sound like a baby, so my first words to my dear wife that morning come from deep, deep in my gullet and sound like " Hello, out there beyond the grey curtain. Is anyone out there who cares about this Medicare recipient? Hulloooooooo."

The curtains part and Karen fills my space. I'm greeted with a warm gentle kiss followed, lest I feel too spoiled, by "God, you need a shave."

Karen looks great in her lavender cashmere sweater set and tailored black slacks, really put together like she sensed that one of us needed to make impressions and decisions and that wasn't likely to be me. I want to gab, to act the silly little boy role that my Dad played so well, but there are bigger issues going on just a few feet away.

Karen holds my hand and we listen together. Suzie is screaming into the phone. I picture an overwhelmed intern at the other end. "Kareem, I need you to get hold of Doctor Benton right now and tell him he must come to Scripps Memorial Room 410B right now to see Michael Streetman." She forces a pause between each word, like she is hoping he is at least writing the details down.

There's a longer pause, then a flicker of uncertainty in Suzie's face as she says, "Well, I'm not technically his wife anymore. Does that matter?" Apparently, it does matter. The flicker in her face expands to stupor. She seems all at once to be a sad, faded parody of the take-charge woman I met only an hour or so ago. Karen leaves my side, snatches the cell phone, and hands it to Mike. His eyes look gray like a GI in a foxhole too long, but he seems to be aware of what's going on. His weak and weary voice contrasts with Suzie's.

"This ... is ... Mike ... please ... tell. ... my ... Doctor ... to ... hurry." And then, to seal the deal, a horrible manufactured scream, which scares the shit out of me even as I see the wry smile on Mike's face.

Tony the Nurse races in and takes charge. "Calm down now Mikey-Boy, I got yer morphine shot right here. And ladies, I need you to be on the far side of this here curtain as I'm closing it." Mike doesn't even get a chance to explain the motivation for his scream before the needle hits his butt. Karen and Suzie go off to have a cup of coffee and discuss how much time to give Dr. Benton before calling again and threatening to sue.

I'm left alone and feeling neglected. I reach for the button, but pushing it seems wrong, even irresponsible, given what's going on with Mike. Instead, I grab the TV clicker and push that button. A housewife in a robe wearing too much mascara is coming on to the conveniently bare-chested gardener. Click. Judge Judy is telling a gum-chewing tattooed punk that marriage used to mean something. Click. Bounty kitchen towel commercial. Click. Two Hispanic guys with boxing gloves in a cage kicking the shit out of each other. Hmm, pretty interesting. They roll over and over, slapping rabbit punches to each other's neck and face until Paco Hernandez finds himself on top and applies the winning choke hold, allowing a break for commercial.

A jowly bearded man wearing a seasoned black Homburg strides into my room. He doesn't bother to knock. He opens his mouth to speak. His incisors are yellow. He thrusts a calloused hand in my direction, apparently seeking a shake. "Rabbi Feldman from Chabad checking to see if your religious needs are being met."

Religious needs? Do I have any? I decide to take control. I accept his right hand in mine, but cover the outside of his hand with my left. Now I'm in the soothing, caring rabbinic position and he's not. "Actually, my own rabbi just left a few minutes ago after attending to my religious needs," I lie.

He's got to be pretty sure I'm putting him on and he's clearly not used to being trifled with. He wants to challenge me but his hand is still enclosed in both of mine. And I'm a hospital patient to boot. "Do you know about the Chabad Movement?" he asks. The tone is suddenly reverential.

He doesn't realize the lollipop pitch he's just delivered to the center of the plate. "Well, actually, my law firm has had some, shall we say, confrontational interactions with your Rabbi Kauffman involving near-death estate-plan changes by alleged Chabad converts."

I part the waters with my hands, allowing his meaty paw to escape. His bravado is gone and he's in full retreat.

"Well, if you'd ever like to talk some more or hear about what Chabad is doing to strengthen our ties to Israel, please call me." He reaches into his suit pocket and pulls out a business card. He chicken-wings the card on the corner of my table farthest away from me, maybe concerned that I might try another handshake, and backs up into the hallway, mumbling to himself in Hebrew. My gaze returns to the television. Danny O'Flaherty in red trunks is pummeling a black guy with dreadlocks. Round two is almost over. I doze.

Karen's soft lips are on my forehead, awakening me. I appreciate the attention, but it's gone in a second. "Mike's doctor will be here in half an hour. I called and pretended I was his wife. He actually spoke to me. Isn't that great?"

Of course, it's great, but what about me?

"Karen My Sweet, you can't believe the number I just did on the Rabbi from Chabad. Fat guy with a beard and a black hat wanted to know if my religious needs were being met in here."

I look for admiration in her eyes but see only concern. "I thought you quit hitting the button. Now you are hallucinating about fat rabbis."

"No, it really happened just a few minutes ago. Weird people are coming to my hospital room all the time, like the skinny old lady with the poodle yesterday. She was actually offended that I didn't want the pampered beast to lick my face."

"And this was all in Chicago, right? Or has your fantasy world perhaps moved to Milwaukee?"

But even as she's saying this, her eye wanders to the near edge of the tired gray tray table where the Blackhat left his card, and further down to a glossier business card with a photo of Fluffy, the Therapy Dog. Karen reads the caption out loud, "Fluffy's kiss can cure the blahs." I begin to laugh, a big belly laugh that hurts my incision. She begins to cry, giant puffy sobs of tension release. Her arms are around my neck now, our faces touching, her wet tears following gravity's path toward my neck. The harder she cries, the more I laugh. We hold the pose for a long time. Someone closes the curtain. I doze.

The curtain is back open when I'm awakened by the scurrying near Mike's bed. Dr. Benton has arrived, two eager Asian interns at his heels. He's tall and big-featured and before he can say a word, I know he's cold and clinical. He's barely concluded the clearly distasteful handshakes with Mike and Suzie when he launches into the speech we've all been waiting for. His tone reminds me of Hal the supercomputer in 2001, A Space Odyssey, before he malfunctioned.

"Mr. Streetman, we have reviewed your case extensively and, subject to one remote possibility which I will refer to later, we feel that amputation of your right leg approximately two-and-one-half inches above the knee and immediate commencement of prosthesis training is the prescribed course of action." He pauses for a millisecond, but continues before the questions can make their way past his patient's lips. "I am available to perform the amputation, which will take approximately three hours, the day after tomorrow at three pm. Do you have any questions?"

I can't believe the asshole doctor actually asked whether they had any questions. Suzie starts to cry. Mike jumps right in. "Why two-and-a-half inches above the knee?"

Just the kind of technical, unemotional question Dr. Benton hoped for, I'm sure of it. He strokes his chin before answering. "It is very important to pick the right place to amputate to maximize blood flows and minimize the risks of infection as well as to assure that a subsequent operation will not be required. We have identified the precise location."

I want to ask who "we" is. Hopefully it's not just this mechanic and his fawning interns. I look at Mike and can't tell whether he's really listening or just readying a follow-up question.

"What kind of artificial leg will I get?" Mike asks.

"That's a topic for a different day. Suffice it to say that modern prosthesis is a science whose time has come and that the available products offer the discriminating purchaser a wide variety of options."

Did he really say 'suffice it to say' and 'discriminating purchaser'?

Suzie's eyes are still red, but the crying is over. The words stumble from her lips. "You ... you ... mentioned a remote possibility."

"Yes, the MRI we have is just a little blurry in one area and I'd like a clearer picture simply to confirm the nerve damage I would anticipate there. Thus, I have arranged for Mr. Streetman to have another MRI later today. But my experience tells me it will not change my conclusions." The interns nod their heads in unison.

Suzie asks the follow-up question I would have asked. "Why wouldn't you get the MRI results before having this conversation with us?"

Benton's all business. "Because I don't have another opening in my surgery schedule for three weeks and you need to make your decisions promptly. Is there anything else you need to ask me?"

Mike shakes his head. Suzie looks at the floor. Benton and his minions wait the appropriate twenty seconds and then leave the room. Suzie starts to cry again. Karen embraces her and absorbs the sobs. And Mike says to nobody in particular, "In one sense, I guess I'm lucky. The right leg he's taking has always been my bad leg. Hell, with the right prosthetic, I might be playing tennis in six months. Can you imagine how fucked I'd be if they had to amputate my left leg?"

I wonder whether I was supposed to hear that. I want to laugh and cry. I bury my head under the covers, assume the fetal position and beg for sleep. They wheel Mike off to Radiology a few hours later. Shortly after he leaves, I'm told that my bed is being moved down the hall to accommodate Mike's wish, made two days earlier, for a private room. I wonder whether he still wants us to leave.

My new roommate is a skinny coffee-skinned teenager with a tiny gold earring who lies on his back and stares silently at the ceiling. A woman who must be his mother sits by the bed; she looks scarcely older than her boy. She's intensely and intently silent. I can almost feel the prayers flowing from her heart into the air above her head. I do not believe, in that first moment, that I will ever converse with this woman.

But my spouse, the inclusive one, has a different take. "Hi, I'm Karen. I guess we'll be sharing this room with you for a while. You look like you need some sustenance. Can I get you a sandwich and a cup of tea from the cafeteria? Or would you like me to just leave you alone?"

Maybe a minute passes before she responds in a tired, beaten voice with just a trace of a Jamaican accent. "I'm not sure I'd feel right about eating till my son can. He's on the intravenous. Attacked by a gang at the bus stop and the knife got into his liver. All I can do now is pray."

And in that moment, all I can do is hit the button.

They released me from the hospital three days later. Me and my walker made a detour to Mike's room while Karen got the car. Mike was in bed, snoring. His ex-wife and daughter were wearing germ-free orange space suits. I gave Suzie a big hug and my card and asked her to keep me informed. I never heard back. My leg still hurts.

Mentor

Ron rolled the worn black documents bag through the narrow aisle of PSA Flight 246, marveling at his own skill at avoiding the knees and elbows of the passengers already seated. He was stoked. He'd spent a week in San Francisco, sparring with the brightest legal and business minds in the country. The three deals he was shepherding through the process had closed, each in the manner most favorable to his client. He had begged, cajoled, flattered and out-maneuvered his adversaries. It was clear from the toasts at today's celebration lunch that he had once again been the star of the show. These very important people couldn't wait to work with him again and looked forward to cutting more fat checks to his law firm, just like the ones he was now carrying in his left vest pocket, close to his heart. 1983 had been a great year for Ron and the firm and there was no reason why 1984 couldn't be better.

Ron wondered whether it was luck or charm that got him selected for the last available seat on the plane. Quite a few others appeared to be ahead of him on the list, but that freckled redhead behind the PSA counter really fell for his not-totally-untrue sick wife story. He was the last passenger to board and ended up in a middle seat in the back row. He snoozed through the takeoff and awoke to the cheery "what may I bring you sir" from the flight attendant to his window neighbor. What a lucky day—the drink service was actually starting from the back of the plane.

Ron swirled his glass and shivered, feeling the Jack Daniels cool as it made contact with the rocks. He knew exactly when the temperature of the oily brown liquor would be perfect to his palate. At that magic time, he took a generous sip, felt the powerful kick, and almost purred. He pulled out last Sunday's New York Times Magazine Section and began attacking the crossword in blue ballpoint ink, filling in the entire square when he was sure of the answer and hedging his bets with smaller letters in the corners of the boxes when his answer seemed iffy. His fingernails still showed off last week's manicure and buffing. He checked the time on his entry-level Rolex and stared admiringly at his diamond-inset gold cufflinks.

The unshaven young man sitting next to Ron swigged a Coors from the bottle and lit a Marlboro. Marlboro had been Ron's brand during those formative smoking days of college and law school. In response to the gory details from the Surgeon General and the lectures from his wife and kids, he had first switched to one of the low tar brands and eventually quit smoking almost three years ago. But this felt like a special time. He turned to his seatmate, "Could this ex-smoker bum a Marlboro?"

The young man's eyes brightened. He immediately shook a cigarette loose from the pack and into Ron's waiting fingers. No sooner had the filter reached Ron's lips than the young man had his tarnished silver Zippo lighter at the cigarette's tip. A great long inhale felt wonderful, strangely liberating. Ron's purr was audible this time.

"Thanks, that really hits the spot. I'm Ron Stewart and I live and work in San Diego? What brings you to America's Finest City?"

"I'm Jeff. I ain't really going to San Diego this time, just meeting my sister Mary at the airport and flying on to Kansas City."

"And why Kansas City during the Midwestern winter?"

Jeff paused, frowned and bit at the cuticle of his middle left finger. Ron wondered if he'd regret asking the question.

"Goin back home for a funeral. My Dad passed away a couple of days ago. He drove his old Ford pickup off a cliff and down a ravine. Had another shouting match with Mom at dinner that night and stormed off to Kelly's Kozy Corner. Eddie Kelly tried to take the truck keys, but Dad ran out, drunk as a skunk, and the rest is history."

"I'm so sorry. Were you and your Dad close?

Again, the telltale pause and another bite at the now-bleeding cuticle. "He was a good guy when he was sober and beat the shit out of me when he wasn't. As I got older, I saw less of the sober guy. I ran away from home when I was 16 and haven't seen him since. I talk to my Mom every couple of weeks. She's a drinker too, but she watches her soaps and passes out on the couch rather than bothering people."

"Where's home for you now, Jeff?"

"Actually Sir, that's a very good question. I'm a gunner in the Army, stationed at Fort Ord up near Monterey. Three weeks ago my wife Joyce up and left me. I lost it and went on a binge in San Francisco for about a week. The MPs arrested me last Tuesday. I was in the brig when I my sister called to say Dad had passed. They gave me a ticket to KC and told me I'd better damn well be back in a week."

"What are they charging you with?"

"Damned if I know. Court martial, discharge, demotion, or a slap on the wrist, I got no clue."

Ron listened, spellbound. He had read novels about trailer trash folks with lives like this, but he had never spoken with one of them. Jeff insisted that he buy a round of drinks. When Ron protested, Jeff's comment was "It's so good to have someone to talk to about these things."

Eventually Jeff's narrative shifted to questioning. How would Ron advise Jeff to handle his problems? Ron was sure he gave the absolutely right answers, only slightly aware of how pompous they sounded.

"Don't duck your problems -- face up to them."

"Cut down on the drinking -- it's only going to get you in trouble over the long haul."

"You've got to decide if your marriage is worth saving -- if it is, you need to tell her that and make the necessary sacrifices."

"You need good legal advice regarding your situation with the Army -- maybe I can make a call or two and help you out if you can get me some more details."

"Do everything you can to re-establish the relationships with your mother and sister."

"Find a way to improve your education -- you're too smart to be stuck in menial jobs the rest of your life."

And Jeff was eating it up. Jeff asked about Ron's kids. Ron proudly described the accomplishments of Peter, who covered the Japan desk for Merrill Lynch, and Kim, now in her second year at Harvard Law School and engaged to one of her classmates. At Jeff's request, Ron whipped out his wallet and showed the family pictures they had taken this past Christmas, each of them wearing identical white polo shirts and designer jeans.

"Do you and the Missus ever fight?"

"We argue all the time, but we make it a point never to go to sleep mad at each other."

"Why couldn't I have parents like that?"

Ron thought he saw a tear in Jeff's bloodshot left eye. Jeff looked away and blotted the damaged cuticle with a cocktail napkin.

Ron loved to watch the plane land in San Diego. Everything was so larger than life, the downtown high rises, the Coronado Bridge, Balboa Park. He leaned over Jeff's seat to get a better angle and his forearm brushed Jeff's knee. The contact was not unpleasant.

"Pardon me, Jeff. I was just trying to get a look at the skyline."

"No problem, Sir. Feel free."

They were the last to leave the plane. Ron pulled a card from his engraved silver card case, wrote on it, and handed it to Jeff.

"Please let me know how things are going at home. Call me on my private line, the number I jotted down in ink. I'll see if I can figure out a way to help you with your legal problems."

They shook hands and Ron thought he detected a quiver in Jeff's throat when Jeff said, "Thanks for listening and really, really hearing me."

***

Ron approached the yellow lead cab on the taxi line. A familiar and unpleasant ritual was about to begin. Ron's car was parked at the office, only a couple of miles away. After waiting on line for an airport fare for an hour or two, the cabbie would be frustrated with the prospect of a $6 fare. Ron was not unsympathetic to the driver's plight, but nevertheless felt victimized.

Ron mumbled "600 B Street, please" and winced at the half audible, stage-whispered "shit" in response. The posted hack license said the driver's name was Stuart Dabney. Stuart reminded him of Jeff, grubby, unhappy, overmatched and without a mentor in a difficult world. Ron attempted conversation, but got the silent treatment from Stuart.

It was not realistic to try to save another soul today. Ron's thoughts drifted back to Jeff's plight. Who could he call on for help? One of the firm's associates had been a JAG lawyer in the Marines—maybe he knew an Army JAG lawyer. Maybe Ron could just make a cold call and use his charm on the prosecutor. Maybe he could find a law school buddy with connections. Maybe...

Ron realized that the cab was approaching his office building and began his internal debate on whether to over-tip or under-tip. The argument for over-tip was to compensate the cabbie for his long wait, since the small fare would not. The argument for under-tip was that surly and non-communicative behavior like Stuart's should never be rewarded.

The cab stopped in front of Ron's building. The meter read $7.50. Ron decided to over-tip and not ask for change for $10. He reached into his pocket for his wallet, but felt nothing but dirty cloth.

We Tried Not To Laugh

We tried not to laugh as we pretended not to watch Stephanie take each possession from her desk and decide whether to pack it or trash it. Now she grasped the tinny bowling trophy with her name engraved under "Ladies First Prize" which she'd won with a spare in the final frame at Company Bowling Night. We remembered her awkward jump into the air and the kick of her multicolored shoe as the last pin went down. We wondered how many moments of elation she'd felt since. We watched as the trophy was lowered into the gray plastic wastebasket next to her panty-hosed left leg, but then retrieved and placed lovingly in one of the moving boxes so thoughtfully provided by the Company for occasions such as this.

We typed on our computers as if we were working and the collective keystrokes provided the tympanic background for the incessant clicking of her cinnamon gum. We could smell the cinnamon from way across the room, or thought we could. We remembered her inspired performance of "Delta Dawn" at Company Karaoke Night, how we cheered and cheered and demanded an encore.

She pulled a framed photograph from the bottom desk drawer. We gasped at the smiling face of George with the sleepy bedroom eyes and the moistened lips. He'd left her for a Vietnamese pole dancer last year. Steph's eyes tensed, like maybe she'd just discovered rat droppings, and we were glad that the security guard was only a few feet away from her, ready to pounce at the first signal of antisocial behavior. She held the picture at arm's length and we could feel the wheels inside her brain clicking in tune with her gum. And then her eyes relaxed a wee bit and she took apart the frame, ripped the picture in half and the halves in half, threw the pieces in the trash, kept the frame, and rubbed her beautiful soft hands together before lowering them again into the bottom desk drawer. We secretly hoped she'd pull out a vibrator next.

We loved Stephanie. We were sure she'd find another job, probably a cushier one with a private office and a great dental plan. But most of all we were pleased the axe had fallen on her and not on ourselves.

Rack of Lamb

I couldn't take much more of Walt's motormouth bullshit. This was the second time tonight I'd heard about the time in Aspen when he'd skied "practically alongside" David Letterman and how he'd told Dave a couple of jokes and Dave had thought he was really funny and maybe there might have been an opportunity for him to audition for the show or some show. "But screw it I was making so much money in real estate at the time that show business really didn't have much of an appeal but now that the bubble has burst maybe I'd try standup but to do that he'd really have to move to LA or Chicago or New York and I just like it too well here in Santa Barbara although on the other hand I'm really pretty flexible now that my former wife's taken the house on the hill and Bank of America has the beach house and I'm housesitting for a friend till the first of next month."

I prayed silently for the main course to come soon—otherwise I was going to have to go to the ladies' room again. Walt had said he was the youngest of five kids and I pictured a dinner table where everyone was starved for attention, trying to get the limelight and this little frustrated tyke was never able to get a word in. I saw him weeping by his bed, with sheets that pictured racing cars, vowing that someday, when he was grown up, people would listen to him, be fascinated by his every word.

"Ah, the rack of lamb pink, just a little pink, for the lady," said the surfer-by-day-waiter whose nametag said Ben, and Walt scowled just a little at the interruption I relished. Walt had that ruddy complexion one associates with yachts and long, slender fingers that gestured too much. I'd met him a couple of years ago at a charity fundraiser and been flattered when he asked for my card and promised to take me out for a spectacular dinner "and a bottle of Pinot that'll knock your socks off."

Two years passed before he called last week, but he wasn't at all apologetic and I accepted his invite all too eagerly. And the wine he had ordered tonight might just have stirred my pantyhose if Walt could just have kept his mouth shut and wooed me with those beautiful blue eyes and long soft eyelashes.

"And the Beef Wellington, medium, with a side of fois gras, for the gentleman," and this time Walt smiled as the plate was lowered before him, apparently delighted with the gentleman reference. The waiter saw there were only a few ounces of wine left and asked whether another bottle was in order and Walt said "But, of course" and I said "Not for me, I've had quite enough, Walt." Walt ignored me and repeated, "But, of course," to Ben and Ben asked deferentially "Are you sure, Sir?" and Walt said, "BUT, OF COURSE." The waiter poured the remaining wine into Walt's glass and hurried off, shaking his head.

At least the lamb was fantastic, five juicy little ribs perfectly seasoned with white pepper and cardamom and mint and maybe just a hint of anise, surrounded by tiny perfect winter vegetables, brussel sprouts and turnips and mini-squashes, fabulously undercooked. I didn't want to share a morsel and was relieved when he didn't ask for a sample.

He'd gulped down the wine in his glass by the time the new bottle arrived and made a great show of sniffing the cork and swirling before tasting, as if he could have known the difference with the amount he'd already consumed. I allowed Ben to refill my glass, not because I wanted more but because Walt might drink less. Walt seemed to be enjoying his food and the silence was exhilarating. I even caught a few snippets of conversation from a nearby table where two sixty-somethings held hands and told revealing stories about their former spouses, seemingly unconcerned about the delays between courses.

Apparently, Walt's tolerance for silence had reached the saturation point. He put down the knife and fork he had wielded so beautifully in the European manner, took a two-ounce gulp of wine and looked at me with those now-cloudy baby blues. "Have yever been to Barthelona?"

I shook my head no and continued my assault on the lamb, sensing an attempt would be made to hold and stroke my greasy right hand if I let go of my utensils.

The words oozed from his mouth now, like they were being forced from a tube of ointment. "Then I wanna take ya to Barthelona and show ya the archifuckingtechture and drink Tempranillo and eat olives and crispy sardines witchoo. Willyacome, willya (and here there was a pause while he tried to remember my name and failed)?"

I muttered an 'excuse me' and left the table. On the way to the ladies' room, I rubbed away the wetness around my eyes and cornered the tuxedoed head waiter. "My date has had a little too much to drink. Please bring him the check while I'm freshening up and clear the plates. And don't let him order dessert. We need to get out of here." He nodded and patted my greasy hand like a nurse humoring an octogenarian.

I guess I stayed in the ladies' room for at least ten minutes, enjoying the luxury of leisurely removal and reapplication of makeup, then washing my hands twice with deliciously warm water as if that would remove the stain of him. I walked back to the table, feeling erect and sober, eager for this abortion of an evening to end. I heard him before I could see him, his words still jumbled together as he told the waiter, "GoddamAmerican-Express can't possibly decline me. I'm fuckinplatinum. Try again and bring me some goddamn cremebrulee."

Ben the waiter was barely subservient now. "Sir, we've talked to two supervisors at American Express and this card has been cancelled. Do you have another card I can run, or perhaps cash?"

I was at the table now although Walt hadn't spotted me. His eyes were looking toward the ceiling, perhaps seeking divine intervention or maybe just trying to avoid the waiter's critical eye. "No more cards and fourteen stinkinbucks in my pocket. But I'm platinum donchasee, I'm fuckinplatinum."

I cleared my throat and he saw me and there was a gleam of recognition when I think he remembered my name. Then he looked up toward the ceiling again as he fed me the bullshit. "Barbara, Barbara, there's been a screwup with the American Express computers. Cudjagivem your card and I'll payya back tomorra, I promisya?"

I eyeballed the tab, $342 plus tax and tip. Each of those bottles of sock-knocking Pinot was 110 bucks. The second bottle was still almost half full. I pulled out my non-platinum Visa and mentally readjusted my budget for the month. All that mattered in that moment was getting out of there and fast.

He managed to find a couple of bucks for the valet and seemed to be handling the car well enough at the start. It was less than a mile to my house and I longed to be there and rid of him. He made a rough stop at a red light and turned to me, his complexion no longer ruddy, his facial features now puffy and indistinct, and slurred "IwannatakeyatoBarthelona. IwannatakeyatoBarthelona." He said it twice as if that would prove his sincerity.

I lost it. I reached over his leg, turned off the ignition and grabbed the car keys, then got out of the car. I shouted "Hey Walt" to make sure he was watching, then reared back and threw those keys as far as I could into the blackness on the side of the road. "Sleep in the car, Walt, and don't call me in the morning" was the best I could come up with as I trudged toward home in the black patent leather heels that matched my purse.

Abe

It was at my seventieth birthday party, eleven years ago. Our Florida friends and relatives, my two daughters and five granddaughters from Scarsdale and New Rochelle and a few nieces and nephews from Queens and Wantagh all came to celebrate that day at my condo clubhouse in Boca. They told stories about me, roasted me a little for my bad posture and my drooling habit, and paid me quite a few compliments. But it was Jerry Fleisher, known for throwing clubs on the golf course and cards at the poker table, who hit my nail on its head.

In that booming baritone of his, Jerry concluded his remarks with, "But most of all, my friend Abie is a people person."

He said it and he was right. I'm a people person. I'm not the smartest guy I know by far and in my prime I was never better than average-looking and I'm certainly no idealist or philanthropist and while I made a comfortable living selling insurance to the Jewish community and an occasional Gentile, I always thought of myself as a good guy who was nothing very special. But now I realize that not only am I a people person, but I am a star people person. People really like me and love to hear my stories.

My people person talents explain why I just got elevated from substitute to regular status at the 5-days-a-week afternoon gin rummy game at Boca Acres. They needed a fifth regular player after Sid Levinsky passed in April. His gout had made him an unhappy man for years.

You gotta hear about these guys at the gin game. There's Arnie, who used to be a major league umpire—no shit—and now he's about as blind as a goddamn bat and makes us play with the cards with the big numbers and letters and still holds them about an inch from his face. About once a day he'll lay down a heart meld with a diamond in the middle or vice versa. One time when he did that, I saw it and stuck my right thumb in the air and screamed, "You're out" and the guys absolutely broke up it was that funny.

Then there's Lenny who really can't hear shit as opposed to the rest of us who can't hear much. I sometimes mouth words around Lenny so that he'll think I'm talking and he can't hear. He realizes what's going on only when everybody laughs at him.

And there's Ed who's got the worst prostate in the history of Florida (or so his doctor claims) and he takes a piss about every ten minutes and sometimes waits too long and that results in a delay of the game while he exchanges one pair of polyester pants for another.

And finally, there's Harry who once was a bigshot estate planning lawyer in Chicago and did the wills for a lot of the Jewish Mafia guys and the Teamster bosses. I'm guessing he was one hell of a gin rummy player in his time but now he's got Alzheimer's and sometimes can't remember what game he's playing.

My wife Rose says I always win, but no I tell her that's not so. It is almost impossible to win when your gin partner that day has Alzheimer's. Nevertheless, Rose can't understand why they keep inviting me back when I win 90°/o of the time. But I know and I tell her, "Rosala, they love me. They love being with me. Remember, I'm a people person."

Rose and I have been together for 58 years, the first two of them in sin. She understands me pretty good, but doesn't always appreciate me. I think lots of other women would find me fascinating if I were ever on the loose.

Being a people person is great when we go on cruises. There's an opportunity for Rose and me to meet hundreds of new friends. I can tell my favorite stories to a bunch of folks who've never heard them and never have to say "Stop me if I've told you this one before" or "Did I ever tell you my story about the time we sat in the first row at a hockey game." And I quickly become the guy everybody on the ship knows and wants to be with.

Like the day we were assigned to a table for four for dinner with this couple, the guy very well dressed and looking like maybe he'd had some work on his face over the years and probably had a personal trainer who came twice a week to his mansion in Malibu or his office in Century City. And she was quite a looker, probably in her late fifties, wearing a glittery top which showed off a lot of well-tanned décolletage. They told us right off they're Sid and Evelyn from LA and that they are not married but are involved in a long-term relationship. I tried to break the ice by asking whether they think the relationship will last all the way to the end of the cruise, but Sid didn't think it was funny at all and Rose found it necessary to apologize for me. Evelyn looked at me like maybe my question wasn't so stupid.

After that we talked about the bond market, the pros and cons of Medicare drug plans, whether the housing market in LA would collapse, and what we planned to do for our three hours of shore time in Gibraltar. I invited them to join us for dinner again, but they said they had bookings arranged for most nights and had scheduled two romantic dinners on the balcony of their suite. He smirked and she blushed.

As he pulled her chair away at the end of the meal, he stroked her ass and she seemed to rub that tuchus right back into his hand. The waiter brought the bills and we each checked our receipts to make sure the drinks got charged to the right person. They did, except I got the bill for the Evian water they ordered and all of us drank. I sensed Sid knew it, too. I decided to be a mensch and not say anything to the cheap bastard.

So, the next morning is a day at sea and I'm scheduled for a class on digital photography and Rose decides she's not feeling so good and she's going to sit and read her Danielle Steele novel and I get there a few minutes early for the class and who's there early too but Evelyn. The two of us are standing in the hallway, waiting for the previous class to clear out and making small talk about breakfast and the cruise director, but I sense this bond between us and know what I have to say. I take her elbow in my hand and look straight into her eyes.

"So, does this guy intend to marry you?"

She looks puzzled. I decide to rephrase. "Has he spoken about marriage with you or is he ducking the issue?"

She whispers back at me. "Neither one of us is interested in another marriage at this time. But we're in a committed relationship."

Sounds like BS to me. I forge ahead. "So, does he take good care of you, buy you nice things, treat you good?"

She tries to pretend she didn't hear and I'm just getting ready to rephrase again when she whispers, "He's good to me. We're good to each other."

I am not convinced. "Because I gotta tell you I sensed last night that your friend Sidney might be a little tight with a buck and I don't want to see a nice girl like you getting hurt."

Her mouth is open as are the mouths of four other soon-to-be photo students who have joined us in the hall. My truth may have embarrassed her. I decide that I've said almost enough. "Let me know if you want to discuss this further. I'm a very good listener and I'm in cabin 6437."

I saw them at the buffet lunch line the next day. When his back was turned, she lip-synched something like, 'I'll be in touch when I can.'

I never heard from her.

He must have been watching her like a hawk.

Too bad.

She needed my help.

Wounds

Frank Jennings shuddered and pulled the collar of the weather-beaten herringbone overcoat up even higher, hearing more than feeling the scrape of the coarse wool against his neck stubble. The gloomy muck of a sunless January 26 in Giuliani's Manhattan was segueing into the bleaker muck of night. He tried a mind trick from his growing-up days, willing his brain to focus on the promise of spring, imagining a warm May sunset, the sheer drama of brightness descending into black. It worked for an instant, yielding a fleeting blessing of warmth. But the chill of his personal reality quickly returned.

Frank had $16.75 in his pocket to cover him until February 1, when the next measly disability payment would arrive in his account at Chase. He was hoping to buy some really cheap food as the Union Square Farmers' Market closed down this evening. He saw prices cut by 25 and even 50% as the afternoon wore on, the foot traffic dwindled and the temperature dove. But this was New York where prices started at outrageous and went up from there. Even with 50% off, nothing was affordable.

Did he have the balls to ask to buy the leftovers at 10% of retail? Was there a difference between asking for a 90% discount and begging? So long as he was paying, it couldn't be freeloading, could it? But his inner CPA wasn't buying the rationale, "What you're really saying is that you want to buy the salad at retail so long as they'll throw in the entree, dessert, beverage, tip and tax for free and that's begging."

A lone snowflake bit his cheek. He brushed it away, feeling the gristly, grimy cheek stubble, surprisingly like the wire brush he'd used on the horses 30-odd years ago. His weight had fallen dramatically since Labor Day. There was little flesh and lots of bone, like those tiny shorthaired dogs at the Westminster Kennel Club finals he'd watched on TV.

Frank approached the Artisan Breads booth. The young man behind the counter was absorbed in the football action emanating from a tiny red transistor radio on the counter. Frank cleared his throat and the man looked up. Frank began the speech he'd been rehearsing, "Sir, I'm a street person who has never been a beggar. I fend for myself, don't make trouble, and don't complain. I'm very hungry and I'd like to buy any leftover bread you choose (except the jalapeno) for 40 cents. I know your bread is marked down already from $5.50 to $2.75, but I can't afford that. I'm sorry I can't pay more." His heart tingled and he felt the adrenaline racing through his empty innards.

The clean-shaven kid with the black wool cap covering his ears took a deep breath. "Sorry Mister, I can't do that. My boss would kill me. We have a company policy--we donate everything we don't sell to charity. But, let me at least offer you a sample. This is our eight grain with fresh figs."

Frank grabbed the two largest chunks in the basket and thrust them into his mouth, the sticky fig fragments clinging to his dry gullet. The questions began multiplying in his brain. Why would this guy rather give a loaf to charity than sell it to me? Because I'm here in flesh and blood, am I less worthy than some fancy charity supported by the rich folks who regularly buy this bread? Are Woolcap and his boss afraid of losing a tax break? Are they afraid I'll do this all the time or bring my unsavory friends? Or are they just reluctant to deal with "people like me"?

He wanted to ask Woolcap all these questions, but instead smiled and tried to sound dignified, "I understand. Thanks for the sample. It was tasty." And the young man turned away and began to pack up his wares.

Frank slumped off, already hungrier than before. He passed an apple display, did some mental math and kept going. The citrus stand was open and there were still six Valencia orange wedges on the sample plate. He grabbed the three biggest, relieved to see the grocer turn away, as anxious as Frank to avoid an incident. Frank's dry, overexposed lips puckered and crackled on contact with the acid fruit.

He smelled spice and took a deep breath to savor the rich perfume of fully ripe stargazer lilies, like a teaser for the Arabian Nights. A pleasant feminine voice said "Sir" and Frank took another couple of steps before he realized that "Sir" must be him. He turned and saw a very fat young woman, probably 200 pounds on a 5-2 frame, wearing bright green wool slacks and a hooded maroon sweatshirt with a Pratt College insignia. She was chewing on a jumbo Snickers bar. A tiny river of chocolate drool was trekking over her considerable chin and crashing down her vast neck. But her voice was soft and lilting, like one hears from a loony character in a play before she goes off the deep end. That voice sure didn't match her body.

"Sir, it appears that my helper has lost his way. I require assistance in packing up my flowers and transporting them to the shop. I can pay $20 for what should amount to no more than two hours' work. And perhaps throw in a bunch of camellias as well."

Frank had done a little acting in his youth. "Madam, I cannot accept your generous offer as made. I must ask that my gratuity be lilies and that it only be payable if my services are exemplary."

Her giant brown eyes blinked twice. "Sir, your counteroffer is accepted. I will require something less than exemplary but more than adequate. My name is Maria Antonelli. What is yours?"

"I'm Frank."

"And your surname?"

"Tyler", he said, lying for no good reason.

She was an efficient and energetic worker. Frank adapted to her cadence. They placed the flowers and plants on the ancient wooden pushcarts and covered them with plastic wrap and thin blankets to keep the stinging wind from penetrating too deep. He insisted on doing most of the bending, handing the potted plants up to her while his knees scraped the pavement.

She looked down and grinned. "Why, Frank, you look strangely religious in that pose."

"Ave, Maria," jumped out of his mouth before he could bite the stifle button.

She thought it was clever and didn't seem at all offended.

Rolling the carts was tougher than loading them. They were poorly balanced, the wheels were small and old, and the sidewalks were anything but smooth. The streets were a little better, but the cabbies and double-parkers forced constant changes of course. Maria led and Frank followed. They frequently shivered and occasionally giggled. It took almost half an hour to navigate the four short blocks to the tiny florist shop.

Unloading was easier. A few extremely perishable items required immediate cold storage, but most others could stay on the cart or the floor until the morning.

Marie glanced at her antique gold wristwatch. "One hundred and four minutes, a new record. Great job, Frank."

"Thank, Maria. And could I use the restroom?"

"Sure, light's on the right wall."

He arched his back and really enjoyed the pee, pleased by the constant thick flow. He waited for the last drip to drop by itself, disdaining his traditional shake. But the twinkle in his eye disappeared when a glance in the grimy mirror revealed the weather-beaten scarred gray face of a homeless guy. All his clever banter couldn't disguise the fact that he was a bum and she was just performing an act of charity. Ave Maria, my ass.

He smelled the lilies as he opened the bathroom door. The twenty was in her left hand and the pink and white bouquet in her right. He took the crisp bill in his hardly-washed left and reached for the flowers with his slightly-damp right. She pulled them back just a little.

"Frank, you've more than earned these flowers, but I've grown quite fond of them myself. Can I buy them back from you? I'm offering home cooked spaghetti and veal meatballs, buffalo mozzarella salad, and a decent Chianti. And a hot bath for you at my place while I cook it all. What do you say?"

His mouth seemed frozen in the open position, like a window left ajar too long in damp weather. From way, way back in his throat came the word yes.

They walked the few blocks in silence. He was winded from the steep climb to her fourth story walkup. She was not. The drafty hallway was barren but clean; there was no evidence of graffiti. She opened the door and the warmth flooded out at him. She must have kept the temperature at 80 degrees all day just to feel this rush of heat on her chilled bones. And this evening he was a beneficiary too. The apartment was tiny, not at all to Maria's scale or the scale of her oversized antique furniture. Everything was green and maroon and patterned. The walls were covered with black and white family photos. "Sicily?" he asked.

"Yes, most of them. This is my favorite, my great-grandparents on the dock waving to my grandparents as they leave for the New World. Sends chills through me still." Chills made her realize how hot it was in the apartment and she turned the thermostat from 81 to 73. She then headed for the linen closet, handing him a maroon bath sheet and a yellow washcloth.

"Take your time in the bathroom, Frank, I've got lots of preparing to do. Do you prefer a bath or a shower?"

"Actually, I was thinking about both. Is that okay?"

"Perfect, and here's a little Chianti starter to take in there with you."

He couldn't believe what emerged from his mouth next. "Maria, do I smell bad?"

"Of course, you do, Frank. But the bath will take care of that. And there's a disposable Gillette razor in the medicine cabinet if you choose to shave. Now enjoy yourself and give me a five-minute warning when you're close to ready."

The giant tub perched on little feet occupied half the bathroom. Frank turned on the nozzles full blast and began slowly undressing, cataloguing the state of disrepair of each clothing item as he removed it. He'd need at least one more wool sock in the very near future. His white tee shirt was falling apart, but he could hold off replacing that till spring. The Eddie Bauer fleece-lined boots, a recent find next to a Park Avenue trash bin, looked a little tired but felt great even though they were a full size too small.

The bath was full enough to enter now and he did so gingerly, being careful not to splash water onto the tile checkerboard floor. The water temperature was perfect. His eyes closed and he took exaggerated deep breaths, secure in the feeling that this intensely pleasurable experience could last for as long as he wanted, that he'd be ready to get out of the tub long before anyone would require him to do so.

He soaped up the oversized yellow washcloth, smelling fresh squeezed lemon, and guided it on its journey over his long bony body, beginning just below the right ear. He encountered cuts and bruises and bites and scabs and a few blemishes he couldn't describe or recall. He was halfway down the right leg when he felt the spot, the place where little bits of shrapnel lingered below the surface, the place the surgeons couldn't get to without damaging the nerve. "Not now, please not now," he heard himself whisper.

But 'not now' never worked anymore and he was back there in that filthy muddy trench, leg bloody and infected, unable to move and facing an equally terrified enemy soldier. Each had an automatic weapon pointed at the other's head.

Only about ten feet separated them. Death for both was certain. The script had been written. He had silently pled for a way out. His adversary had slowly nodded his head as they locked eyes. Each released an iota of pressure on his trigger finger, then another iota and another. The young Vietcong soldier took a tiny backward step, then another, then still another.

The gunsights remained fixed and each trigger finger was ready to move at the slightest sign that the other was violating their silent pact. The youth was at the top of the trench now and allowed a tiny smile to cross his face as he made an awkward farewell wave with his non-gun hand. And then the brutal rat-tat-tat-tat of automatic fire, lots of it, and the Asian was not a person any more, only guts and blood, lots of blood. And someone was shouting to Frank, "Nice work holding him off, soldier. The medics are on their way. You're gonna be fine."

Frank screamed as he did most nights, a long wailing scream which started in the eye sockets and ended deep in the leg where the shrapnel was buried.

Maria was outside the bathroom door. "You okay, Frank?"

"Sure, just banged my knee getting out of the bath. I'll be out in ten minutes or so."

He had no idea what could happen next.

A Recipe For Changing

Changing a light bulb in the bedroom closet demands a wide variety of skills and close judgment calls.

First there's the issue of which ladder to use. The big seven-footer is the popular choice, but the long winding trek from garage to bedroom typically results in both a pulled shoulder muscle and a major ding in the hallway stucco. The small stepladder is easier to transport and would most certainly be the right selection for 99% of the adult population of the Western World. But if you've been Guinness-certified as having the world's shortest arms, those same shoulder muscles will pay the price during stepladder bulb-changing. Nevertheless, you choose the stepladder.

Place stepladder under dusty fixture in closet. Begin unscrewing the three screws which hold the filthy glass globe. Those screws are invariably too tight and at an awkward angle, making leverage almost impossible. You're at the point where you curse the asshole who overtightened those screws last time and then realize that the asshole was you.

Somehow the fixture finally comes loose and you have to juggle it before gaining control. It is filled with dust balls and semi-decomposed insects, many of which resemble dust balls. Descend the ladder with the fixture in tow and proceed to the sink. Clean the fixture with warm water and soap like your mother taught you; then wash your hands, being sure to remove the dragonfly wings from under your fingernails.

Dry fixture and set aside.

Return to closet and turn on light switch. Observe which bulb is out. Turn off light switch and ascend ladder. Remove defective bulb without burning fingers and descend. Check wattage on bulb and trek to garage cabinet to find correct replacement bulb. During return trip to bedroom, wonder why replacement bulbs for bedroom closet aren't kept in bedroom closet.

Ascend ladder with replacement bulb and screw in.

Descend and turn on light switch to confirm that new bulb works. Ascend ladder holding bug-free fixture in left hand. Use right hand to loosen the three screws a little more. If you need to switch hands, it is strongly recommended that you do so on the ground and not on the ladder. Carefully place domed fixture in its setting and begin screwing screws, alternating among them. Your shoulder will ache, but tough it out even when the angles seem impossible. And just when you think you have failed, the fixture will hold. It is recommended that you smile at this point, just before you realize you have once again overtightened the goddamn screws.

God, this was so much easier when there were two of us.

Magda's Place

It was a relief to smell 14th Street after the potpourri of puke, stale beer and a day's worth of farts that had pervaded the Lexington Avenue Express. Not that Union Square was the Hills of Tuscany in springtime, but at least the rotting lunches in the trash barrel and the cheap cigar smoke were somewhat neutralized by the cold damp winter air whipping cross-town from the East River.

I'd been in the office from 8 until 7, with only a noontime tuna on Kaiser roll (extra mayo, no pickle) to tide me over. I hadn't peeked into my refrigerator for a couple of days but was pretty sure there was nothing satisfying in there, unless I wanted a Rolling Rock appetizer and Corona for the entree. Chinese takeout jumped into my head, as it invariably did. But this would be the third night in a row and there was something vaguely unsettling about how well Ming and Lee were getting to know my likes and dislikes and the extra egg roll or gratis cup of soup I'd occasionally find in the bag.

Pizza, maybe. But pizza raises all sorts of issues. Do I get a whole pie, knowing I couldn't come close to finishing it? What would be wrong with carefully wrapping the uneaten pieces in aluminum foil and having them there to reheat and scarf down a couple of nights from now? There was no reason why my fridge couldn't be more than a beer and orange juice cooler. But ordering a whole pie would mean waiting at the drafty pizza stand for 15 or 20 uncomfortable minutes, making awkward conversation with the greasy-haired kid with the incredible biceps behind the counter. Much easier to get a couple of slices, even if they weren't as fresh and were never as crisp as I liked.

"Give me five bucks and I'll tell you something that'll change your life" rasped upward from next to my loafers. I looked down and saw an ugly old woman, a caricature out of a comic book. A raspberry-red rash dominated her small round face. There were boils on her neck. Her ankles were so swollen there was no sign of bone. She was dressed in rags and shards of blanket, except for a surprisingly clean and newish bright purple headdress that covered whatever hair might be left on her head. I wished the headdress could somehow have covered up her facial hair—she had whiskers and a little tiny goatee for Christ's sake.

I almost never give money to beggars although I'm not sure why. If pressed, I'd probably fall back on the argument that giving simply encourages those people to beg, exacerbating the problem for them and for us. Deep down, I think this is bullshit and occasionally beat myself up for not answering the plea of some poor soul who I'm convinced really would buy soup and not Thunderbird with my couple of bucks. I looked up and took a step away from her.

"I ain't beggin. I'm offrinya a great deal. You couldn't buy what I'm sellin for a thousn dollars." It was like she had read my mind. Her voice was soft, scratchy, and faintly Middle European, yet every syllable came through unmistakably clear. As she talked, she tugged firmly at my pants cuff from her seated position on the sidewalk. "I'll not let you resist easily," her gloved hand was telling me.

I used to think five dollars was a lot of money and my parents still do. I thought of walking away, with the hope that she'd offer me the info for less, but that seemed chickenshit. I could almost feel the hook imbedded into the inside of my cheek-- I had to know what she wanted to tell me. I reached into my wallet and saw I had three singles and three twenties. I showed her the contents of my wallet, wondering whether she'd take the singles or change the twenty. "Go get five", she grunted and pointed to a candy store down the block.

A slovenly old man smoked his pipe behind the counter, and I knew right away that free change for a twenty was not in the cards. I fingered several candy bars before settling on a Toblerone with hazelnuts for $1.75. Before approaching the counter, I slipped a twenty from my billfold and returned the wallet to my pocket, not wanting to reveal to the cashier that I did in fact have smaller bills. "Nothing smaller?" he mumbled, and I shook my head, hoping he'd accept my lie. He did. I walked out, put a five in my left hand and shoved the rest of the change and the candy into my right pocket.

I looked down the street. The woman was not there. Her patch of sidewalk was vacant. I felt my throat constrict.

"Don't panic, I'm right here," she said. She was standing next to me, no more than five feet tall, at least 175 pounds and wrapped in gray army/navy store blankets and that incredible purple headdress. I smiled down at her and handed her the bill. She tucked it between some folds and advised me to listen carefully and follow her instructions.

"When you leave me, walk straight to the corner of Fourteenth and Broadway. When you get there, check your watch. Walk south one block. At the next corner and at every other corner, walk whichever way your legs tell you to go. When you have walked for exactly 19 minutes, find the nearest ethnic restaurant and go in. Your life will never be the same."

I was confused. There were so many questions I needed to ask. "How will I know where my legs want to go? What do you mean by ethnic? What happens if I don't immediately see a restaurant? How will I know I found the right place?"

She raised her right hand and tenderly touched my face. Her dirty arthritic index finger had broken through the weathered woolen mitten. I was surprised that I didn't flinch.

"Trust and all will happen. Destiny awaits you. Begin your voyage from the everyday." It sounded like a Star Trek soundbite.

She turned to walk away. I touched her shoulder. I think she expected more questions from me. Instead, I handed her the candy bar. She smiled and I realized there were only two teeth to attack the Toblerone. I began the trek to Broadway.

I'm not a very spontaneous person. At the first corner, I wasn't at all sure how to figure where my legs wanted to go. After a long pause, I thought they chose west, but halfway down the block I had doubts. But at each subsequent corner it got a little easier to let go and trust. My pace quickened as I zigzagged through the narrow, non-linear streets of the West Village. At the magic nineteenth minute, I was on a tiny residential street and looked in vain for a neon restaurant sign. I continued walking in the same direction and saw an old brownstone, four stories tall with massive bay windows on each floor, the kind of place a robber baron might have built in the early 20th century. At the front door, a single uncovered 60-watt bulb faintly illuminated a small unadorned sign that said "Magda's."

I'd found the place. I turned the brass handle and entered a long, dark hallway. Stuffed heads of wolves, foxes and other forest animals sneered at me from the mahogany walls and kept me on a straight path. There was light at the other end of this tunnel. And the light had a name, Magda.

She greeted me with a warm, full-body hug and a loud, throaty, "Velcome to Magda's." Before I could utter a single syllable, she continued, "You must never tell me your real name. Make up a name and we'll always call you that at Magda's. Close your eyes right now and don't open them until you have a name you truly like."

I obeyed. With eyes shut tight, I realized that Ralph Davis wasn't much of a name. I opened my eyes to look around, but Magda was staring at me and my lids flicked down instantly. What about Harry Stanton, Peter Granger, Karl Essenoff, or Solomon DeMarco? I could be Harrison Peterson, Taggart Whipple, or Jeffrey (or even Geoffrey)

Coolidge. Why not Percy Chubb or Garfield Heard or Porter Davenport? So many choices, so little time.

And then I had it. I opened my eyes and looked straight at Magda. "My name is Derek Twain and I'm delighted to meet you," I said in my most elegant voice. And without any premeditation or anxiety, I took her hand, brought it to my lips, and gently kissed it.

She smiled and maybe even blushed a little. "What a pleasure to have you with us this evening, Mr. Twain. If you were planning to dine alone, may I offer you the alternative of joining the head table?"

My head was saying no, but nodding yes. And what came out of my mouth was even more remarkable, "And please do call me Derek. Mr. Twain seems much too formal."

She led the way, making a sharp left turn into the dining room. I was not prepared for its enormity or opulence. There were perhaps a dozen banquettes, a half-dozen isolated tables for two, and an imposing head table in the center, capable of seating at least twenty. There were about 12 at the table that night, all elegantly dressed. The men wore jackets and ties or ascots, and the women sported expensive-looking dresses, high heels, and glittering bracelets. Fred Astaire and Ginger Rogers would have fit in. My wrinkled khakis, Doc Martens, and checked lumberjack shirt felt itchy and bulky and all wrong.

Then Magda, the perfect hostess, announced to the group, "This is Mr. Derek Twain, who we are delighted to have with us for the first time. In my opinion, he's one of the handsomest bachelors to sit at the head table this season. He'll be sitting at my side this evening."

The wine flowed about as freely as the conversation. I was delighted to discover that I had opinions to voice on every topic that was discussed, from the upcoming mayoral election to the latest exhibition at the Guggenheim to the plucking weaknesses of the new concertmaster of the Philharmonic. I found I could be pithy or witty or outspoken, but I was always charming and in control. When I spoke, others at the table strained their ears to listen. I reciprocated, trying to wring every glimmer of meaning and every nuance out of each comment I heard.

The food was incredibly good. We began with a salad of shredded beets, tiny cold Brussels sprouts, miniature pearl onions, and Gorgonzola crumbles, with a dressing that tasted vaguely of black figs. The soup was the clearest, most flavorful consommé I'd ever tasted. This was followed by a baby veal paprikash, served over a potato-based pasta I can only describe as firm gnocchi. All three servers (two women and a man) were in tuxedos and glided around the table, attending efficiently and effortlessly to our needs.

I told Magda I had no room left for dessert. "You must try our honey date tart," she responded. Extraordinary streusel dough, fresh honey and Medjool dates laced with a pear brandy combined to wear down my resistance. I even ordered a second slice with my tawny port and espresso, not realizing that a plate of rich butter cookies would accompany the after-dinner drinks.

I'd been at the table for about three hours when the check was slipped onto the table to my left. I felt a stab of panic, realizing that the meal and all its accompaniments could set me back $200 or more. It wasn't that the money was an issue, but more the WASP guilt for spending on myself that my parents had instilled in me. I squinted at the check, which was handwritten in a language I didn't understand, but had a bottom line of $65. Delighted, I whipped out my American Express card and placed it on top of the bill.

Magda put her hand on mine and whispered into my ear, "Unless your credit card is in the name of Derek Twain, it's no good here." I loved the ear tingle and got the message, even before she followed up with, "Seriously, we only accept cash from our guests. If you don't have the cash with you, just bring it next time. I know you'll be back." I squeezed her warm hand in gratitude, hoping it might encourage another throaty whisper. It didn't and it was time to leave.

She led me through the narrow hallway toward the front door, then pulled me aside into a dimly lit alcove. She handed me a business card, which contained only the name "Magda's", the address and a phone number. She told me to call when I wanted a reservation or to simply drop in alone any evening I felt like it. I was never to share the phone number or address with anyone else. I could only bring a single guest at a time (and then only if the guest had been pre-approved by Magda at the time the reservation was made). Her demeanor became sterner as she recited each requirement and she sounded downright Germanic when it culminated with, "And deez are de rules of Magda's Place."

It sounded so rigid, quite the opposite of my evening's experience. Yet it didn't seem right to challenge her and I had no immediate plans to bring a guest anyhow, at least as long as there was a possibility of being Magda's seatmate again.

I slept through the night and awoke without the hangover I had every right to expect after drinking 20 ounces or so of red wine and a big glass of port. I was at the office by 7:30, incredibly energized and engrossed in my spreadsheets. I slipped out at noon and brought back a giant takeout container of wonton soup, which I wolfed and slurped down at my desk in about three-and-a-half minutes. I burped and then pulled the card from my pocket, a part of me afraid that the ink might have disappeared. It hadn't. I dialed the number and Magda answered halfway through the first ring.

"Magda, it's Ralph Davis from last..." was as far as I got.

The Germanic voice again. "I don't know any Ralph Davis," she blurted, and the next thing I heard was a click.

My throat constricted. Then I realized that Magda really didn't know Ralph Davis—her customer was Derek Twain. I hit the redial button, but quickly hung up; afraid she'd know for sure that it was Derek who had violated the rules. I told my computer to bleep me at 4:30 with a reminder to call Magda and forced myself back to work. It wasn't easy to wait for the bleep but I did.

"Magda, this is Derek, Derek Twain. I so much enjoyed last evening and was wondering if there was a seat for me at the main table tonight." I sounded so sophisticated and genuine at the same time.

"My dear Derek, it vill be our pleasure to entertain you once again zis evening. Please be here by eight. Ve're opening a magnum of 1961 Dom Perignon. And if it isn't too much of an inconvenience, dress up for dinner. Several of the young ladies have speculated about how you'd look in a cashmere double-breasted blazer and an Armani tie."

I left the office at 6:30, whistling. The subway was overflowing with ugly humanity, but it didn't faze me. I raced up the stairs at 14th Street, anxious to see my gypsy benefactor, but she was not there. I hung around for ten minutes or so, hoping she'd been taking a leak or something. No luck. I stopped at the ATM and withdrew $300 in crisp twenties, knowing I had two meals to pay for and not sure what the Dom Perignon surcharge might be.

After one more careful look for the lady with the purple headdress, I went home. I luxuriated in a hot bath, shaved, slapped on my favorite aftershave, and selected and put on each article of clothing more carefully than I knew how. This was about as far away from grunge as it gets.

I knew where I was going this time and was very aware of the most direct route. Nevertheless, I decided to return to 14th Street and retrace my original journey. I hoped to see the Gypsy Woman and wondered whether she would notice and comment on my spiffy outfit. On my way to 14th Street,

I bought a white carnation and had the flower girl expertly insert it in the loophole of my blazer. Foppishness was fun.

The Gypsy wasn't there. I thought about asking one of the other blanketed homeless on the corner where she might be and if she was okay But I wasn't sure how to describe her in words that weren't insulting, and I knew that a donation would be expected and wasn't sure what amount would be appropriate but not excessive. I trudged off, following the previous night's sacred route to Magda's. Only once along the way did I wonder whether the restaurant would still be there.

"Derek, you look fabulous. I simply love men who display flowers. It shows a remarkable confidence in their manhood, I think." Magda was wearing a white silk dress with a plunging neckline. I waited for her to turn her head so I could stare down the middle, but her eyes were riveted on me.

"Magda, you are radiating with beauty tonight. And I hope you won't be offended if I remark that only a truly feminine woman could wear your dress with aplomb."

What am I saying? I don't talk like this.

She giggled and placed her arm in mine. Her skin was incredibly soft. "I knew immediately that you vere a charmer. And I'm sure I vill catch you peeking quite a few times this evening. Let's have a glass of Dom, shall ve." Sometimes the accent was there and sometimes it wasn't.

The group numbered twelve when I entered, but quickly grew to about 25. A few of the faces were familiar. Everyone was good-looking, even the most senior citizens who were old enough to be my parents. Almost every woman I spoke with fondled my boutonniere. The champagne was wonderful, but the hand-passed caviar crepes were even better. Magda was the perfect hostess yet kept returning to my side. When the bells were tingled for dinner, she directed me to the head of the table and allowed me to seat her at my side.

I was once again more charming than I'd ever been. Magda didn't monopolize me, but she was right there beside me, with those beautiful boobs beckoning. She brushed against me several times and it sure didn't seem accidental. And once, in response to a touching childhood story I told, she gently stroked my outer thigh.

I suppose I drank too much wine with dinner and I know I should have declined the second glass of port. But everything was so wonderful, so bigger than life, that I lost all sense of proportion and restraint. Eventually, I looked around and saw the only three remaining guests settling their bills. I found mine and was pleased to discover that this dinner cost only slightly more than the previous one. I left payment for both plus a very generous tip.

"Shall I escort you to the door?" Magda asked and took my arm without waiting for a reply. My forearm met her cleavage for only a millisecond before she readjusted her hold. My heart was jumping by the time we got to the front door. She put her arms around my neck and planted a soft gentle farewell kiss on my right cheek, mumbling at the same time, "Thank you for coming, Derek."

My arousal and the alcohol took control. I planted my lips onto hers and tried to force her mouth open with my tongue. Her resistance was immediate and emphatic. She pulled away and said dismissively, "No, no, no, you'll spoil everything."

"I don't want to spoil anything. You are the most exciting woman I've ever known and I think you like me a lot. Can't we let go?"

"No, we can't. Good night, Derek." She had turned to ice. She opened the door and firmly pushed me outside into a downpour. There was not a cab in sight and after walking three blocks, it didn't seem to make sense to hail the one that finally appeared. In just a few moments, I had been transformed from the City's most charming and self-assured man to a sopping-wet depressed drunk.

I felt like shit the next morning and didn't get to the office until 10. I kept replaying the gestures and the dialogue. Hadn't she led me on? Wasn't she making it clear that she cared for me and had picked me out for her special attention? Maybe I had just scared her with my outburst of passion. Or maybe it was important to her that she be wooed on her own terms, away from the restaurant. That must be it.

My hands were shaking as I dialed her number. I'd rehearsed the speech in my head over the lunch hour, but totally forgot it when she answered the phone with her throaty, "Magda's."

"Magda, this is Derek. I'm really sorry that I disappointed you last night and desperately want to make it up to you. Can I take you to the opera and dinner tomorrow evening?"

And she hung up.

I dialed again, but the phone just kept ringing. I left the office at four and went right to the restaurant without freshening up. I rapped on the door and heard her shout, "Go away, Ralph." I kept rapping until a cop came and told me to move on if I didn't want my ass hauled off to jail. I moved on.

I called later that night and got a recording saying that the number had been disconnected, "and there is no new number." I wondered how the regulars would make their reservations.

I saw the Gypsy Woman the other day. She wouldn't talk to me either.

Mostly Untrue Stories